ACCSE 2017

The Second International Conference on Advances in Computation, Communications and Services

June 25 - 29, 2017

Venice, Italy

ACCSE 2017 Editors

Pascal Lorenz, University of Haute-Alsace, France
Jos Trienekens, TU Eindhoven, the Netherlands

Printed from e-media with permission by:

Curran Associates, Inc.
57 Morehouse Lane
Red Hook, NY 12571

Some format issues inherent in the e-media version may also appear in this print version.

Printed by Curran Associates, Inc. (2017)

International Academy, Research, and Industry Association (IARIA)
412 Derby Way
Wilmington, DE 19810

Phone: (408) 893-6407
Fax: (408) 527-6351

petre@iaria.org

Additional copies of this publication are available from:

Curran Associates, Inc.
57 Morehouse Lane
Red Hook, NY 12571 USA
Phone: 845-758-0400
Fax: 845-758-2633
Email: curran@proceedings.com
Web: www.proceedings.com

TABLE OF CONTENTS

ACCSE 2017

Forward

The Second International Conference on Advances in Computation, Communications and Services (ACCSE 2017), held between June 25-29, 2017 in Venice, Italy, continued a series of events targeting the progress made in computation, communication and services on various areas in terms of theory, practices, novelty, and impact. Current achievements, potential drawbacks, and possible solutions are aspects intended to bring together academia and industry players.

The rapid increase in computation power and the affordable memory/storage led to advances in almost all the technology and services domains. The outcome made it possible advances in other emerging areas, like Internet of Things, Cloud Computing, Data Analytics, Smart Cities, Mobility and Cyber-Systems, to enumerate just a few of them.

The conference had the following tracks:

- Spatio-temporal Analysis for Smart City

We take here the opportunity to warmly thank all the members of the ACCSE 2017 technical program committee, as well as all the reviewers. The creation of such a high quality conference program would not have been possible without their involvement. We also kindly thank all the authors that dedicated much of their time and effort to contribute to ACCSE 2017. We truly believe that, thanks to all these efforts, the final conference program consisted of top quality contributions.

We also gratefully thank the members of the ACCSE 2017 organizing committee for their help in handling the logistics and for their work that made this professional meeting a success.

We hope that ACCSE 2017 was a successful international forum for the exchange of ideas and results between academia and industry and to promote further progress in the areas of computation, communications and services. We also hope that Venice, Italy provided a pleasant environment during the conference and everyone found some time to enjoy the unique charm of the city.

ACCSE 2017 Chairs

ACCSE Steering Committee
Carlos Becker Westphall, Federal University of Santa Catarina, Brazil
Mario Freire, University of Beira Interior, Portugal
Avi Mendelson, Technion, Israel
Young-Joo Suh, POSTECH, Korea
Michael Hübner, Ruhr-University of Bochum, Germany
Sotirios Kentros, Salem State University, USA
Albena Mihovska, Aalborg University, Denmark

ACCSE 2017
Committee

ACCSE Steering Committee

Carlos Becker Westphall, Federal University of Santa Catarina, Brazil
Mario Freire, University of Beira Interior, Portugal
Avi Mendelson, Technion, Israel
Young-Joo Suh, POSTECH, Korea
Michael Hübner, Ruhr-University of Bochum, Germany
Sotirios Kentros, Salem State University, USA
Albena Mihovska, Aalborg University, Denmark
Shigeaki Tanimoto, Chiba Institute of Technology, Japan

ACCSE Industry/Research Advisory Committee

Daniel Ritter, SAP, Germany
Hiroaki Higaki, Tokyo Denki University, Japan
Danda B. Rawat, Howard University, USA
David Nelson, University of Sunderland, UK

ACCSE 2017 Technical Program Committee

Markus Aleksy, ABB AG, Germany
Harald Baier, Hochschule Darmstadt / CRISP, Germany
Carlos Becker Westphall, Federal University of Santa Catarina, Brazil
An Braeken, Vrije Universiteit Brussel, Belgium
Francesco Calimeri, University of Calabria, Italy
Juan-Carlos Cano, Universitat Politecnica de Valencia, Spain
Robert Charles Green, Bowling Green State University, USA
Gabriel Falcao, IT / University of Coimbra, Portugal
Stefano Ferretti, European Space Agency / European Space Policy Institute, Austria
Mario Freire, University of Beira Interior, Portugal
Hong Fu, Chu Hai College of Higher Education, Hong Kong
Veronica Gil-Costa, National University of San Luis, Argentina
Carlos Guerrero, University of Balearic Islands, Spain
Sofiane Hamrioui, University of Haute Alsace, France
Rui Han, Institute of Computing Technology - Chinese Academy of Sciences, China
Hiroaki Higaki, Tokyo Denki University, Japan
Michael Hübner, Ruhr-University of Bochum, Germany
Sergio Ilarri, University of Zaragoza, Spain
Ilias Iliadis, IBM Research - Zurich, Switzerland
Taeho Jung, Illinois Institute of Technology, USA

Copyright Information

Information Ranking in Real-Time for Summarizing Emergency Calls

Jae Kwan Kim, Myon Woong Park, Laehyun Kim
Center for Bionics
Korea Institute of Science and Technology
Seoul, Korea
emails: {kimjk, myon, laehyunk}@kist.re.kr

Keonsoo Lee
Medical ICT
Soonchunhyang University
Asan, Korea
email: keonsoo@sch.ac.kr

Abstract—**Summarizing emergency calls needs to be processed in real-time. Before a conversation is over, the value of a newly acquired statement should be determined. At the same time, the objective of the call, which is to obtain the information on the emergency situation, should be achieved. In this paper, a method of information ranking in real-time is proposed. This method summarizes an emergency call by extracting keywords and calculating the weights of the keywords with their frequency and relations with other words. The keywords are sorted with the weights and assigned to properties of a dialogue model. From the constructed dialogue model, statements which are not related to the conversation's topic can be pruned.**

Keywords-information ranking; summarization; emergency call; real time.

I. INTRODUCTION

One of the most important contributions of summarizing documents is the reduced complexity for human understanding. With the help of technologies in storing and compressing data, the size of documents especially text based documents is free from the requirement for summarization. However, as the meanings of data are revealed when recognized by humans, acceptance by human is one of the most important criteria for evaluating the value of the data. Most summarizations, which are automatically executed by machines, are worked on completed documents such as articles, news, essays, and books. However, in real world, summarizations are performed for documents in progress. Students note key sentences in lectures. Reporters sum up addresses in press conferences. A debater needs to analyze the opponent's opinion and respond to it in real-time. The same restriction exists in responding to emergency calls.

In order to confirm the correct situation of the emergency, the call receiver needs to control the dialogue to acquire the required information. When a conversation loses the point, it should be interrupted and returned to the original objective. In this paper, we propose a summarization based information ranking method. As this method summarizes and determines the topic of an unfinished document, it can be properly applied to report emergency calls which require prompt response before the conversation is over.

The rest of this paper is organized as follows. Section II describes the types of summarization and the dialogue model as background. Section III proposes the main idea of this paper. Section IV concludes this paper.

II. BACKGROUND

A. Summarization

The types of summarization can be classified as shown in Table I [1]. Three criteria are used to identify types of summarization. One is the level of expressions [2]. The expressions in a summary can be either reused from the original document or rewritten. Another is the coverage of summarization [3]. Determining what is important in the original document depends on a viewpoint. Reflecting on the viewpoint makes for a different summary. The other is the number of documents [4]. A summary of series and a summary of an event are different.

The proposed method is classified as a query-based extraction summary for a single document.

TABLE I. TYPES OF SUMMARIZATION

Category	**Types of Summarization**	
	Name	***Description***
Level of expressions in summarization	Extraction Summary	Important words or sentences from the original document are extracted and the set of such keywords becomes the summary.
	Abstraction Summary	Novel expressions are written by analyzing the extracted keywords semantically. Concept generalization, Part-Whole replacement, Metonymy, and Semantic unification are the examples of generating abstraction.
Coverage of summarization	Generic Summary	All the information in the original document are included in the summary.
	Query-based Summary	Only the information which is related to the given query is included in the summary.
Amount of documents	Single Document	Summarization is performed on a single document.
	Multiple Documents	Summarization is performed on a set of documents.

B. Dialogue Model

Every conversation, even a chitchat, has its objective. The objective is achieved by sharing information. Dialogue Model is a structure of information to be shared in the conversation [5]. It consists of six components such as *Who*, *What*, *How*, *Why*, *When*, and *Where*. When dealing with emergency calls, *Who*, *What*, and *Where* are mandatory. Even though the additional information such as *How*, *Why*, and *When* is useful to make more reliable and accurate plans for rescue teams, the *Who*, *What*, and *Where* information is enough to send rescue teams to the scene where the emergency situation occurs.

The summarized result is assigned to fill the properties of the dialogue model. By comparing the relations among properties, the conversation can be saved from getting off topic.

III. METHOD

The proposed method consists of three steps, as shown in Figure 1. Summarization is performed with the first step and the second step. In the first step, keywords are extracted from the newly given statement. The keywords are composed of nouns, verbs, adjectives which are used as a complement, and a preposition. In the second step, the weight of each keyword is calculated. This calculation is executed with heuristic rules. There are three fundamental rules. One is that higher frequency corresponds to higher weight. Another is that the keywords in the same sentence share the weight. The last is that the query related keywords have higher weight. As the objective of responding to emergency calls is to acquire information on the situation of the emergency, what is not related to such objective does not have to be summarized. The third step is constructing a dialogue model with the keywords which are sorted with their weight. As described in Section II.*B*, *Who*, *What*, and *Where* are filled on the preferential basis. The prepositions, which are collected in the first step, are used for determining the sluts of the dialogue model. The constructed dialogue model is evaluated for closing the conversation. If the conversation is not over, a new statement is added and the process is repeated.

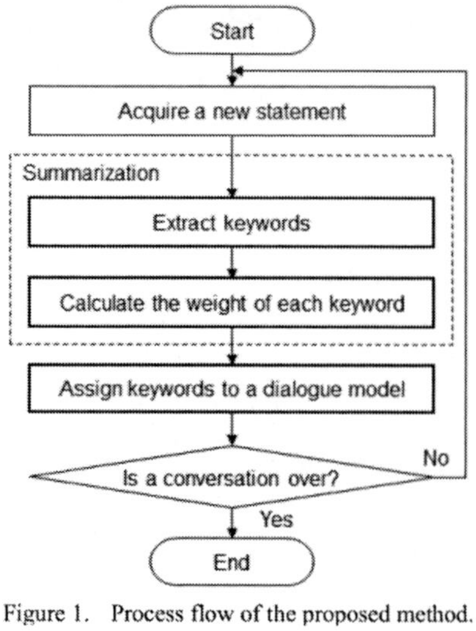

Figure 1. Process flow of the proposed method.

IV. CONCLUSION

Every behavior has its objective. Any behavior which loses its objective or fails to achieve the objective is removed or replaced by another behavior. The objective of emergency calls is to notify the situation and ask for help. In order to achieve this objective, it is important to extract valuable information and evade the wasteful usage of time and efforts. Summarizing a conversation is a key for determining the worth of each sentence. In this paper, a method of information ranking in real-time is proposed. This method summarizes an emergency call by extracting keywords and calculating the weights of the keywords with their frequency and relations with other words. The set of keywords are sorted with the weights and they are assigned to properties of a dialogue model. From the constructed dialogue model, statements which are not related to the conversation's topic can be pruned.

This method assumes that the newly added information is in a grammatically correct form. However, formal sentences are not made in a real conversation. In order to process such broken, ambiguous, and unfinished sentences, a reliable natural language processing module is needed. Thus, the way of processing informal statements will be researched as future work.

ACKNOWLEDGMENT

This work was supported by the ICT R&D program of MSIP/IITP. [2015-0-00197, Development of a solution for situation-awareness based on the analysis of speech and environmental sounds]

REFERENCES

[1] A. Nenkova and K. McKeown, "Automatic Summarization," INR, vol. 5, no. 2–3, pp. 103–233, Jun. 2011.

[2] M. R. Amini, N. Usunier, and P. Gallinari, "Automatic Text Summarization Based on Word-Clusters and Ranking Algorithms," in Advances in Information Retrieval, 2005, pp. 142–156.

[3] H. Saggion, K. Bontcheva, and H. Cunningham, "Robust Generic and Query-based Summarisation," in Proceedings of the Tenth Conference on European Chapter of the Association for Computational Linguistics - Volume 2, Stroudsburg, PA, USA, 2003, pp. 235–238.

[4] D. R. Radev, H. Jing, and M. Budzikowska, "Centroid-based Summarization of Multiple Documents: Sentence Extraction, Utility-based Evaluation, and User Studies," in Proceedings of the 2000 NAACL-ANLP Workshop on Automatic Summarization, Stroudsburg, PA, USA, 2000, pp. 21–30.

[5] K. Lee, J. K. Kim, M. W. Park, L. Kim, and K. F. Hsiao "A Situation-based Dialogue Classification Model for Emergency Calls," in Proceedings of the 2017 International Conference on Platform Technology and Service, 2017, pp. 196-199.

Customer Involvement in Scaled Agile Framework Implementations

Towards a Conceptual Model as a Basis for an Industrial Case Study

Jos. J.M. Trienekens
Faculty Management Science and Technology
Open University
The Netherlands
jos.trienekens@ou.nl

Hatta B. Himawan
Faculty of Industrial Engineering
Eindhoven University of Technology
The Netherlands
hatta.bagus.himawan@student.tue.nl

Jan van Moll
Philips Health Tech
The Netherlands
jan.van.moll@philips.com

Abstract—**The Scaled Agile Framework (SAFe) has emerged over the last years as an approach which supports the improvement of software and systems development. Several software companies have reported on success stories regarding the implementation of SAFe. SAFe claimes solutions for business challenges, such as shortening cycle's times, improving product quality, increasing team members' satisfaction, and involving the customer in product development. However, regarding customer involvement, there is limited research, both in SAFe and in real-life agile software development projects. This study aims to develop a conceptual customer involvement process model as a basis for case studies in industrial companies which are implementing SAFe. As such, this study reflects work-in-progress, and our conceptual model can be considered as a partial achievement of a longer-term research project.**

Keywords- **SAFe; Conceptual model; Customer involvement.**

I. INTRODUCTION

Software development companies have a lot of challenges nowadays. "They need to deliver software in time, within the budget, and within the quality and functional requirements" [8]. The traditional way of software development is not suitable for the development of large scale and complex systems. Agile is nowadays a popular development approach [7]. Agile has proved to be able to handle large-scale complex systems by using several methods and techniqes [14]. Although the Scaled Agile Framework (SAFe) is rather new, some success stories on implementation have already been reported [20]. Although customers issues can be recognized in SAFe, there is limited research on how to involve customers in real-life agile projects [18]. Customer involvement is an essential factor for developing successful software products [17]. However, often companies are not supported in identifing and selecting the right customer types and the customer skills that are needed. Consequently, customers cannot be assigned appropriately in the various development processes, and their performance cannot be measured. For instance, a customer can have essential knowledge of a product, but can lack authority in development processes to decide for particular product features [15]. Also, customers cannot have sufficient time to participate in software development processes [11]. This can cause declining customer motivation and loss of customer interest to get or stay involved in software development, and in SAFe implementations. SAFe considers user feedback and the usage of intrinsic customer knowledge as key for a successful application [10]. Customers are considered as having a critical role in the various aspects of SAFe implementations [18]. However, although SAFe addresses customer involvement issues in its framework, there is limited research done on how to determine and evaluate customer involvement. There are currently no clear concepts and guidelines to involve customers on the various SAFe levels and in the processes. In Section 2, some related work will be discussed. Section 3 focuses at a literature review and analysis. A conceptual customer involvement model will be introduced in Section 4, to support a case study research on SAFe implementations. This customer involvement model will be based on findings from a structured literature research, and will contain guidelines for application during SAFe implementation projects. Section 5 will finalise the paper with conclusions.

II. RELATED WORK

The Agile Manifesto emphasized the importance of customer collaboration in one of its four pinciples [4]. Also in Scrum and ScrumXP, customers should have responsibilities, for example in review and feedback processes [19]. The SAFe framework covers both organizational levels and processes for agile development practices, see the "4-level view" in http://www.scaledagileframework.com/. Four organizational levels can be recognized in this framework, respectively the Team Level, the Program Level, the Value Stream, and the Portfolio Level. Although SAFe states that customers should be empowered in processes such as requirements management, defining solutions, planning, demonstration, and product evaluations [11], it does not provide explicit guidance for employing customer involvement, for example with respect to the type of customer to be involved, in what specific activities, and the customer's barriers to overcome [9]. Since pressure on customer involvement and satisfaction has been increased in the current era [3], new approaches for involving customers should be developed. Customers have to be engaged effectively and efficiently into software development and SAFe implementation projects, and barriers have to be overcome.

III. LITERATURE AND ANALYSIS

Three literature domains provided a basis for our literature search, see Fig. 1. This figure shows the Scaled Agile Framework domain as the main research area, and the highly relevant intersections between the three domains. This study strives at a conceptual customer involvement model for SAFe implementations as an 'integrated concept' of the three recognized domains.

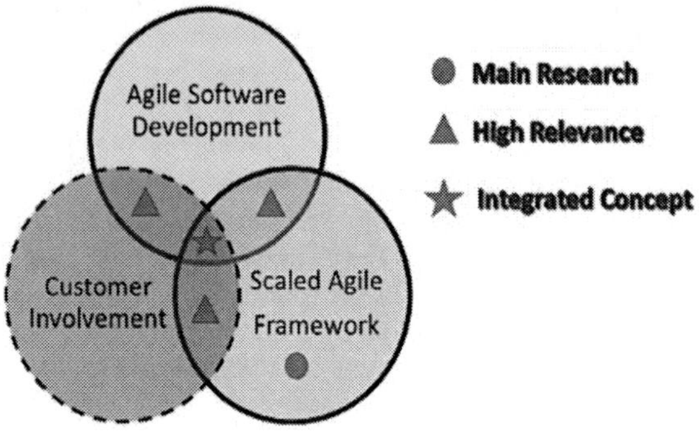

Figure 1. Literature domains.

Regarding the literature on the Scaled Agile Framework, customer involvement is addressed on four levels, respectively: Team Level, Program Level, Value Stream, and Portfolio Level [18]. Analysis results are presented in Table I. Program level and Value Stream are merged because customers have similar activities on these levels, and some activities are closely linked. As can be seen in Table I, customers should be involved significantly at the Program Level and the Value Stream. Most activities are related to validate the product quality in order to meet the customer needs. On the other hand, customers contribute less at the Team Level and seem to not contribute at the Portfolio Level. Regarding the literature domain of agile software development, see Fig. 1, the structured evolution of agile methods has been investigated, see for example [1]. Customers should have an important role in software development processes, e.g., as product owner with critical tasks, such as defining product features, reviewing features, and providing feedback [19]. In the literature domain of customer involvement, see Fig. 1, four main aspects have been identified, respectively: customer role, customer knowledge, customer motives and customer interaction [17].

TABLE I. CUSTOMER INVOLVEMENT ACTIVITIES IN SAFe

SAFe Level	Customer Involvement Activities
Portfolio	-
Program & Value Stream	Evaluating the full system produced, and giving feedback
	Contributing in estimating scope, time, and other constraints
	Attending program increment planning to create the plans for upcoming program increments (PI's)
	Contributing in defining a roadmap, milestones, and releases
	Participating in inspection and adaption (I&A) and workshops to improve next PI's performances
Team	Contributing in creating user stories Performing functional & system acceptance testing at the end of iterations

Three roles have been identified: customers as a resource, customers as co-creators, and customers as users [13]. Regarding customer knowledge, two factors are considered: usage and technology knowledge [12]. On that basis three types of customers are being defined: respectively: ordinary users, experts, and lead users. Regarding customer interaction, literature reports on advances in internet and technology which have changed current product development practices [2]. For example, Nambisan [13] suggested that companies need to design and use virtual customer environments (VCE's) to optimize customer knowledge acquisition and exchange.

Next to these customer involvement issues that SAFe implementations have to deal with, barriers and threaths have also been identified and reported in literature, see [5][16]. Six barriers have been identified in this study, respectively: team diversity (that hinders knowledge exchange, e.g. because of geographical and time differences), team attitudes and values, team competences, team communication, and customer interaction and technology infrastructure.

IV. CONCEPTUAL CUSTOMER INVOLVEMENT MODEL

Based on the literature study and analysis we developed our customer involvement model to help companies to engage customers and to optimize their 'involvement value'. Our model consists of five stages, see Fig. 2. Because customer involvement can increase project uncertainty, the first stage addresses the identification of risks in the project. In stage 2, the result of the project risk identification is used for the determination of the customer involvement level in the project. To support this stage, customer involvement concepts, such as customer roles (i.e., resource, co-creator, user) [13], and customer knowledge issues have to be applied. Subsequently, the next three stages follow an approach for involving external parties, as developed in [21]. These are respectively, a specification, a selection, and a customer value optimization stage. The latter stage replaces the contract agreement stage of [21] because in our study legal aspects are out of scope. The motivation for the latter stage is that it has the same goal as contract agreements, i.e., it ensures that external parties (i.e., customers) perform in accordance with company expectations.

Figure 2. Conceptual customer involvement model

V. CONCLUSIONS AND FUTURE WORK

This preparatory study represents a partial achievement of a longer-term project, i.e., the development of a conceptual customer involvement model to improve SAFe implementations. The conceptual model is based on a structured literature review and analysis. Five stages have been developed and have been elaborated on the basis of findings from literature. The conceptual customer engagement process model will be applied on the short term in an in-depth case study, in Company X. In this company, medical embedded software development is carried out in large evolutionay software development projects. Currently SAFe is being implemented in this company in various projects in different departments and business units. Customer involvement is considered in this company as a challenging and promising area in SAFe implementations. In our case study, we will use an inductive approach, i.e., carrying out semi-structured interviews, document studies and team work observations. Regarding the quality of the case study we will address validity (internal, construct and external) and reliability aspects [22]. Based on the case study results we will strive towards an extended, customer involvement oriented, SAFe framework.

REFERENCES

[1] P. Abrahamsson, J. Warsta, M. T. Siponen, and J. Ronkainen, “New directions on agile methods: a comparative analysis”. In Software Engineering. In *Software Engineering, Proceedings. 25th International Conference,* pp. 244-254. IEEE, 2003.

[2] J. R. Dahan and P. Hauser, “The virtual customer,” Journal of Product Innovation Management, vol 19, no. 5, pp. 332-353, 2002.

[3] U. Eklund, H. Olsson, and N. J. Strøm, “Industrial Challenges of Scaling Agile in Mass-Produced Embedded Systems”. In: International Conference on Agile Software Development, Springer International Publishing, pp. 529–551, 2014.

[4] M. Fowler and J. Highsmith, The agile manifesto. Software Development, 2001.

[5] S. Ghobadi and L. Mathiassen, Perceived barriers to effective knowledge sharing in agile software teams. Information Systems Journal, vol. 26, no. 2, pp. 95-125.

[6] A. Griffin and A. Page, “PDMA success measurement project: recommended measures for product development success and failure”. Journal of product innovation management, vol. 13, no. 6, pp. 478-496, 1996.

[7] I. Jacobson, “What They Dont Teach You about Software at School: Be Smart”! In: International Conference on Agile Processes and Extreme Programming in Software Engineering, Springer Berlin Heidelberg, pp. 1-4, 2010.

[8] R. J. Kusters, L. Pouwelse, H. Martin, and J. J. M. Trienekens, “Decision criteria for software component sourcing: steps towards a framework”. In: Proceedings of the 18th International Conference on Enterprise Information Systems (ICEIS 2016), pp. 580-587, Rome, Italy, 2016.

[9] J. Laage-Hellman, F. Lind, and A. Perna, “Customer involvement in product development: an industrial network perspective”. Journal of Business-to-Business Marketing, vol. 21, no. 4, pp. 257-276, 2014.

[10] M. Laanti, “Characteristics and Principles of Scaled Agile”. In: International Conference on Agile Software Development, Springer International Publishing, pp. 9-20, 2014.

[11] D. Leffingwell, “Agile software requirements: lean requirements practices for teams, programs, and the enterprise”. Addison-Wesley Professional, 2010.

[12] P. Magnusson, “Exploring the Contributions of Involving Ordinary Users in Ideation of Technology-Based Services”. Journal of Product Innovation Management, vol. 26, no. 5, pp. 578-593, 2009.

[13] S. Nambisan, “Designing Virtual Customer Environments for New Product Development: Toward a Theory”. Academy of Management Review, vol. 27, no. 3, pp. 392-413, 2002.

[14] T. Nilsson and A. Larsson, “Agile in Large-Scale Development Workshop: Coaching, Transitioning and Practicing”. In: International Conference on Agile Processes and Extreme Programming in Software Engineering, Springer Berlin Heidelberg, pp. 196-197, 2009.

[15] S. Nerur, R. Mahapatra, and G. Mangalarai, “Challenges of migrating to agile methodologies”. Communications of the ACM, vol. 48, no. 5, pp. 72-78, 2005.

[16] E. Olson and G. Bakke, “Implementing the lead user method in a high technology firm: A longitudinal study of intentions versus actions”. Journal of Product Innovation Management, vol. 18, no. 6, pp. 388-395, 2001.

[17] T. Sauvola, et al., “Towards customer-centric software development: a multiple-case study”. In: *Software Engineering and Advanced Applications (SEAA), 2015, 41st Euromicro Conference,* IEEE, pp. 9-17, 2015.

[18] Scaled Agile Framework, Retrieved from http://www.scaledagileframework.com/, 2016.

[19] K. Schwaber and M. Beedle, Agile Software Development with SCRUM. Prentice-Hall, 2002.

[20] O. Turetken, I. Stojanov, and J. J. M. Trienekens, "Assessing the adoption level of scaled agile development: a maturity model for Scaled Agile Framework." *Journal of Software: Evolution and Process,* DOI: 10.1002/smr.1796, 2016.

[21] A. J. Van Weele, “Purchasing & supply chain management: analysis, strategy, planning and practice”. Cengage Learning EMEA, 2009.

[22] R. K. Yin, Case study research: Design and methods. Sage publications, 2013

Monitoring of Health-Recovery Processes with Control Charts

Olgierd Hryniewicz and Katarzyna Kaczmarek-Majer

Systems Research Institute, Polish Academy of Sciences
Newelska 6, 01-447 Warsaw, Poland
Email: {hryniewi,K.Kaczmarek}@ibspan.waw.pl

***Abstract*—The paper presents a statistical process control method for monitoring health-recovery processes described by short non-stationary time series. The Shewhart control chart for residuals, based on model averaging approach, is built for differences between values of consecutive observations. The practical applicability of this new approach has been demonstrated using a real-life example of a recovery from a mild hypertension episode.**

Keywords–E-health; Control chart for residuals; Short time series; Non-stationary process; Stability of recovery process.

I. INTRODUCTION

Stability is an important feature of many processes. A process is considered stable, or under control, when its uncontrolled variation is purely random (e.g., due to random measurement errors). In 1924 W. Shewhart introduced a simple tool for monitoring stable processes - a control chart. In its initial stage, which is assumed to be in-control, monitored process characteristics are measured, and their mean value and standard deviation are recorded. These recorded values are used for the design of a control chart, known as the Shewhart control chart, which consists of control lines: central, and two (or one, when only deviation of a process level in one direction is interesting) control. The central line represents the mean value of the process level (or a certain target value for this process), and control lines are located at three standard deviations from a central line. The process is considered stable when its future observations are located inside control lines (limits). When an observation falls outside the control lines, an alarm signal is generated, and the process is considered as being possibly out of control (unstable). When a monitored process goes out of control, it is recommended to look for the reason of this, and take appropriate actions with the aim to revert it to the in-control state.

Basic control charts, used in over 90% practical applications, are designed under two main assumptions: statistical independence of consecutive observations, and the normal distribution of measured characteristics. However, in many practical cases, especially when individual process observations are monitored, these assumptions are not fulfilled. Thus, in the recent 40 years, many inspection procedures that do not rely on these assumptions have been proposed. They are usually described in scientific journal papers or in a few textbooks on statistical quality control, such as a famous book of Montgomery [1]. Some of these procedures have been applied in health-related services, and similar applications. A comprehensive review of different applications of control charts in health-care and public-health surveillance can be found in the paper by Woodall [2]. Since the time of the publication of this paper, many other papers on this topic have been published, mainly in journals related to medicine. For example, some recent applications of control charts in the analysis of health-related data can be found in [3].

Despite real popularity of control charts in many areas, such as industry, finance and business, the number of their applications in health care is relatively small. Probably the main reason of this situation is incompatibility of basic assumptions used for their construction, and the reality of health care. For example, consecutive observations of health-related characteristics are seldom independent. Moreover, they are often described by non-stationary random processes, and the runs of interesting observations are short. Therefore, control charts described in popular textbooks, and in the great majority of scientific papers, are not appropriate for monitoring such processes. Some new, more appropriate, approaches have been investigated quite recently. For example, the properties of control charts used for short runs for autocorrelated, but stationary, data have been discussed in [4].

In this paper, we are interested in a special kind of medical data, namely describing health-recovery processes. For many years, physicians have been prescribing certain treatments, and advances in the health recovery of a treated patient have been monitored during visits, e.g., in health care units. Therefore, possible failures of applied treatments were usually disclosed with delay. In many cases, such delays have had detrimental effects on patient's health. However, with the development of e-health systems based on telemedicine this situation has been dramatically changed. Nowadays, it is possible to monitor the state of patient's health even continuously. However, the main problem now is not related to measurements and transmission of data, but to processing of available information. When human's life is endangered, very expensive systems, e.g., in intensive care hospital units, are used. However, in many cases, the usage of all those sophisticated Information Technology (IT) systems is not necessary. It is quite sufficient to process data off-line, and to signal only these cases when consultancy or intervention of a physician is really needed. What is important in this context, it is the stability of health-recovery processes, understood as non-existence of abnormal and unpredictable changes of the monitored process. It has to be noted here, that an unstable process may be still inside some "normal limits", pre-established by physicians, but its revealed instability suggests the possibility of going beyond such limits. Monitoring of such stability can be achieved by the usage of appropriately designed control charts. The proposal of such monitoring processes, based on a control chart for so called residuals, is the main purpose of this paper.

The proposed approach is general, and may be applied in

various contexts. For example, it is suitable to monitor the stability of the blood pressure measurements for patients suffering from hypotension, and to generate early warnings of the Acute Hypotensive Episode (AHE), in which patient's arterial blood pressure decreases to an abnormally low level, that may lead to severe complications or even death. Accurate long-term prediction in this case would allow doctors for timely and effective intervention. The 10th Annual PhysioNet/Computers in Cardiology Challenge 2009 was devoted to predicting the AHE. The results of this competition have been described in [5]. Its participants provided various complex solutions, including: neural networks [6], a rule-based approach [7], decision trees [8] or support vector machines [9]. A short review of other recent approaches for the AHE prediction can be found in [10]. The main aim of all those solution is to predict accidents of AHE for patient in intensive care hospital units. Thus, complex algorithms requiring large computational power could be implemented for this purpose. However, none of them focuses on the monitoring of stability of the processes, and generation of early warnings. The control-chart-based approach, proposed in this paper, yields such early warnings that the stability of the monitored process is disturbed, and that an abnormal episode may occur. Moreover, the proposed method can be easily implemented using limited computational resources.

The paper is organized as follows. In Section II, we describe a mathematical model of a stochastic process (a time series) that may be useful for the description of health-recovery data. Then, in Section III, we propose a control chart based procedure that may be used for monitoring non-stationary health-recovery processes. The problem of the monitoring of short time series using the sXWAM chart, proposed by us in [11], is considered in Section IV. The paper is concluded in its last section.

II. Mathematical Model of a Monitored Process

Consider a real-life example of blood pressure measurements of a patient who is under treatment against mild blood hypertension. In Figure 1, we present results of one-a-day measurements for a period of 480 days.

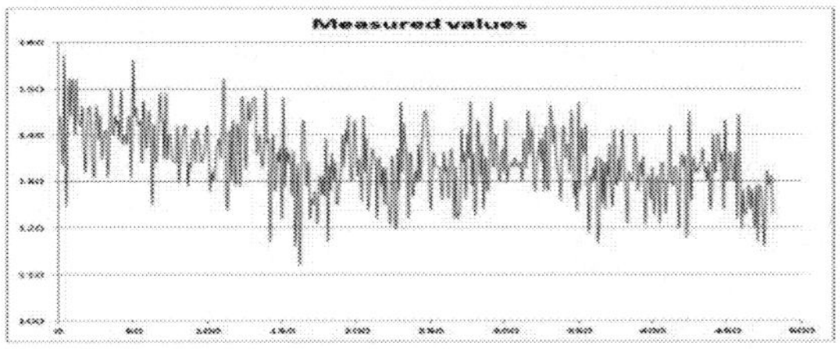

Figure 1. Measurements of blood pressure.

A specialist in time series analysis will find immediately that these measurements, because of a visible trend, may be described by a non-stationary time series (most frequently used methods of the statistical analysis of time series can be found, e.g., in the book by Brockwell and Davis [12]). An important model of such time series is the Autoregressive Integrated Moving Average (ARIMA) model, introduced in the seminal book by Box and Jenkins [13]. For an ARIMA non-stationary process of first order, differences between consecutive observations are described by a stationary Autoregressive Moving Average (ARMA) process, well described in many statistical textbooks. Now, let us look at Figure 2, where such differences are displayed. The process displayed in Figure 2 is definitely stationary. We have found that it may be described by an autoregression process of the fourth order $AR(-0.862, -0.713, -0.358, -0.207)$. Therefore, this real-life example has motivated us to consider in this papers time series described by models of a similar type.

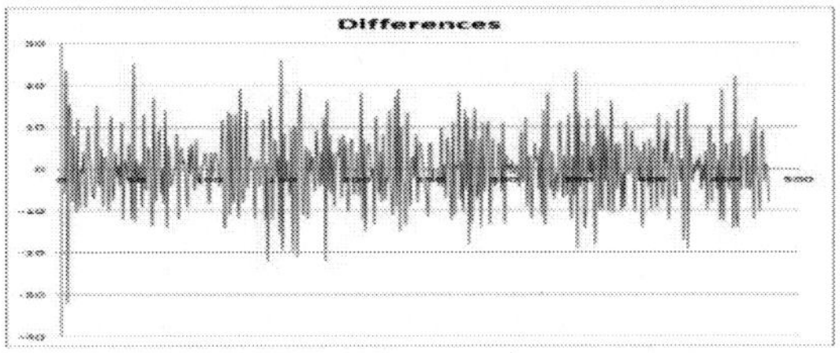

Figure 2. Differences between consecutive measurements.

Let $X_1, X_2, \ldots, X_n$ be a series of measurements obtained during a period of time when a monitored process may be considered (e.g., according to a physician who supervises the treatment) as stable. The process of first differences is now defined as follows: $D_i = X_{i+1} - X_i, i = 1, \ldots, n-1$. We assume the ith difference is related to the previous observations according to the equation

$$D_i = a_1 * d_{i-1} + a_2 * d_{i-2} + \cdots + a_p * d_{i-p} + \epsilon_i, i = p+1, \ldots, \quad (1)$$

where $\epsilon_i, i = p+1, \ldots$ are normally distributed independent random variables with the expected value equal to zero, and the same finite standard deviation.

Estimation of the model $AR(p)$, given by (1), is relatively simple when we know the order of the model p. In order to find estimators $\hat{a}_1, \ldots, \hat{a}_p$, we have to calculate first p sample autocorrelations $r_1, r_2, \ldots, r_p$, defined as

$$r_i = \frac{n \sum_{t=1}^{n-i} (d_t - \hat{\mu})(d_{t+i} - \hat{\mu})}{(n-i) \sum_{t=1}^{n} (d_t - \hat{\mu})^2}, i = 1, \ldots, p, \quad (2)$$

where n is the number of observations in the sample (usually, it is assumed that $n \geq 4p$), and $\hat{\mu}$ is the sample average. Then, the parameters $a_1, \ldots, a_p$ of the $AR(p)$ model are calculated by solving the Yule-Walker equations (see, [12])

$$\begin{aligned} r_1 &= a_1 + a_2 r_1 + \ldots + a_p r_{p-1} \\ r_2 &= a_1 r_1 + a_2 + \ldots + a_p r_{p-2} \\ &\ldots \\ r_p &= a_1 r_{p-1} + a_2 r_{p-2} + \ldots + a_p \end{aligned} \quad (3)$$

The estimators obtained by solving the Yule-Walker equations are, unfortunately, not numerically stable, especially for small sample sizes. A better method was proposed by Burg. A good description of Burg's algorithm can be found in [14]. Burg's algorithm is used to solve the following optimization problem: for the set of observations $x_1, \ldots, x_N$ find the values $a_1^*, \ldots, a_k^*$ that minimize F_k defined as

$$F_k = \sum_{n=k}^{N} (x_n - (-\sum_{i=1}^{k} a_i x_{n-i}))^2 \quad (4)$$

The estimators of the $AR(p)$ model given by (1) are obtained by setting $k = p, N = n, x_i = d_i, i = 1, \ldots, n-1$, and $\hat{a}_i = -a_i^*, i = 1, \ldots, p$.

In practice, however, we do not know the order of the autoregression process, so we need to estimate p from data. In order to do this, we define a transformed random variable, called the *residual*. In the case of autoregression processes, considered in this paper, the residual is defined as

$$Z_i = D_i - (a_1 d_{i-1} + \ldots + a_p d_{i-p}), i = p+1, \ldots, n. \quad (5)$$

When we know exactly the autoregression model, the probability distribution of residuals is the same as the distribution of random variables $\epsilon_i, i = 1, \ldots$ in (1), and its variance can be used as a measure of the accuracy of predictions of future values of the process. For given sample data of size n, the variance of residuals is decreasing with the increasing values of p. However, the estimates of p model's parameters $a_1, \ldots, a_p$ become less precise, and thus the overall precision of prediction with future data deteriorates. As the remedy to this effect, several optimization criteria with a penalty factor, which discourages the fitting of models with too many parameters, have been proposed. In this research we have used the criterion proposed by Akaike [15], and defined as

$$\begin{aligned} BIC = \; & (n-p)\ln[n\hat{\sigma}^2/(n-p)] + n(1 + \ln\sqrt{2\pi}) + \\ & p \ln[(\textstyle\sum_{t=1}^{n} d_t^2 - n\hat{\sigma}^2)/p], \end{aligned} \quad (6)$$

where d_t are our transformed process observations centered in such a way that their expected values are equal to zero, and $\hat{\sigma}^2$ is the observed variance of residuals. The fitted model, i.e., the estimated order p and parameters of the model $\hat{a}_1, \ldots, \hat{a}_p$ minimizes the value of BIC calculated according to (6). We will use this model in the construction of a control chart for monitoring health-recovery processes.

III. Control Chart for Process Monitoring with Autocorrelated Data

A. Design of a chart

The design of a simple Shewhart control chart, in the case of a sufficiently large number of individual and mutually independent observations, is extremely simple. One has to collect data (a sample) from a period when the monitored process is stable, calculate average value $\bar{x}$ and standard deviation σ_x, and set the control limits, upper (CUP) and lower (CLO), to

$$\begin{aligned} CUP &= \bar{x} + 3\sigma_x \\ CLO &= \bar{x} - 3\sigma_x. \end{aligned} \quad (7)$$

When process deterioration is related only to increase (decrease) of a process level, one can use one-sided control charts with respective upper (lower) control limits. Usually, it is assumed that the monitored characteristic is normally distributed, and in this case the probability of observing the observation outside one control limit when the monitored process is stable (i.e., observing a false alarm) is very low, and equals 0.00135. It means, that the expected number of observations between consecutive false alarms is equal approximately to 740 (for a one-sided chart), or to 370 (for a two-sided chart).

When consecutive observations of a monitored process are statistically dependent, the situation becomes much more complicated. For example, when sample data are autocorrelated, the properties of a control chart designed using a simple algorithm described above may be completely different from those observed for independent data. To cope with this problem, statisticians have proposed two general approaches. In the first one, we chart the original data, but control limits are adjusted using the knowledge about the type of dependence. In the second general approach, originally introduced by Alwan and Roberts [16], a control chart is used for monitoring residuals. Their methodology is applicable for any class of processes, so it is also applicable for the autoregression process of differences D_i considered in this paper. According to the methodology proposed by Alwan and Roberts [16], the deterministic part of (1) is estimated from sample data of n elements, and used for the calculation of residuals according to (5). Then, these residuals are used for the construction of our control chart according to the algorithm described above.

It is worth noticing that the Shewhart control chart for individual observations, also known as the X chart, is not the only control chart used for monitoring stability of monitored processes. However, it is the simplest one. Moreover, it is easy to interpret by non-specialists. This second feature seems to us very important if we have to use it in a simple health-care monitoring procedure.

B. Operating procedure

Operating procedure of the proposed control chart for residuals, applied for differences between consecutive observations of the monitored process, is the same as in the case of a classical Shewhart control chart. Using the estimated process model, we calculate the predicted value of the difference between the next two observations of the monitored process. An alarm signal is generated when an observed residual (difference between an observed and predicted values) falls beyond control lines. In Figure 3, we present a one-sided (with an upper control limit) control chart for residuals calculated for the process of differences between consecutive measurements of blood pressure displayed in Figure 1. The model of the process of differences D_i was estimated using first 20 observations of the monitored process of blood pressure measurements. Using Burg's algorithm we found that it is the autoregression process of the fourth order $AR(-0.987, -0.805, -0.217, -0.133)$ (Note, that this model is different from the model estimated from larger amount of data presented in Figure 2). Then, residuals calculated for differences $D_5, \ldots, D_{19}$ have been used for the design of a control chart with the upper control limit equal to 20.29. The estimated model has been used for the calculation of residuals related to the next 80 observations. These residuals are displayed on the control chart. We can see

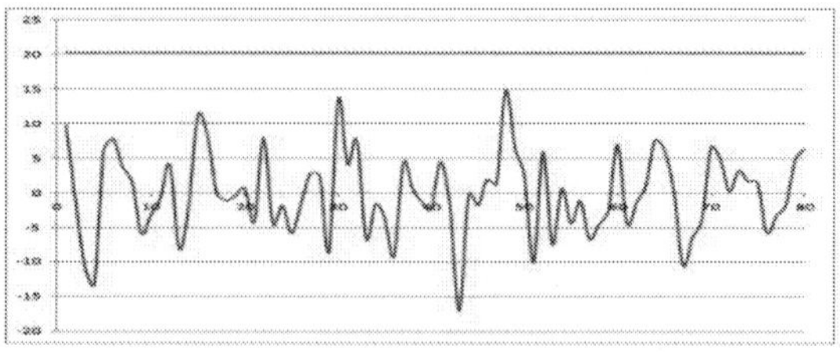

Figure 3. Control chart for residuals of differences of the first order related to measurements of blood pressure.

that the monitored process seems to be under control, as all calculated residuals are located below the upper control limit.

In comparison to a classical control chart for original observations, a control chart for residuals of differences has one important disadvantage: self-adaptation to a changed pattern of data. In order to explain this feature, let us transform our exemplary data by adding 20 to each observation starting from the 10th. The control chart in this case is presented in Figure 4. From Figure 4, we can see that starting from the 10th point

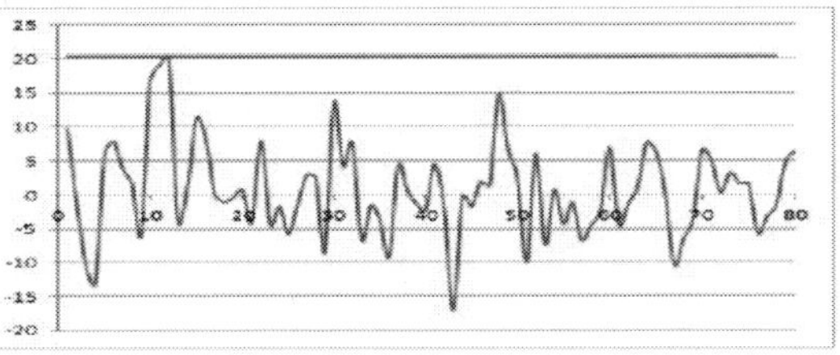

Figure 4. Control chart for residuals of differences of the first order related to measurements of blood pressure with a shifted process level.

until the 12th point on the chart the value of displayed residuals sharply increased, but does not exceed the control limit. Later on, it has returned to the previous level. It means that our chart is able to detect shifts of the monitored process only immediately after the jump. This is in sharp contrast to the classical Shewhart control chart (if it can be applied), where all data points observed after the shift indicate the deterioration of the monitored process. Thus, if the alarm is not generated immediately it will be generated in the future quite randomly, despite the obvious deterioration of the monitored process. Therefore, we have to add an additional mechanism that will increase the probability of detection just after the shift.

One of possible solutions of the problem mentioned above is to use an additional control chart. It can be a control chart for residuals calculated for second order differences defined as $D2_i = X_{i+2} - X_i$. The methodology for the design of this chart is exactly the same as that already described in this paper. Additional advantage of this approach is due to a fact that differences of the second order decrease or even cancel the impact of short cycles in the observed time series. A "weak" alarm signal is generated if it is generated on only one of these two charts. A "strong" alarm signal, that detects possible persistent deterioration, is generated when two consecutive points on the second chart are located beyond its control limits.

In our numerical example of shifted data, the model of the time series of differences of the second order, estimated from the sample of 20 observations, is the autoregression process of the second order $AR(-0.444, -0.555)$. Using this model, we can calculate residuals and design a respective control chart, presented in Figure 5. We can see that in the case of this control chart, deterioration of the process has been revealed with a delay of one measurement. Thus, if we have used both charts, we would detect the change of the process.

Another possible solution which is simpler for implementation, but theoretically less justified, is to calculate an additional residual as the difference between the observed difference of the second order and the predicted difference of the first order, but calculated for the previous observation, and to plot the maximum of these two residuals on the chart designed for the case of differences of the first order. A "weak" alarm is generated when a point on the chart is located beyond the

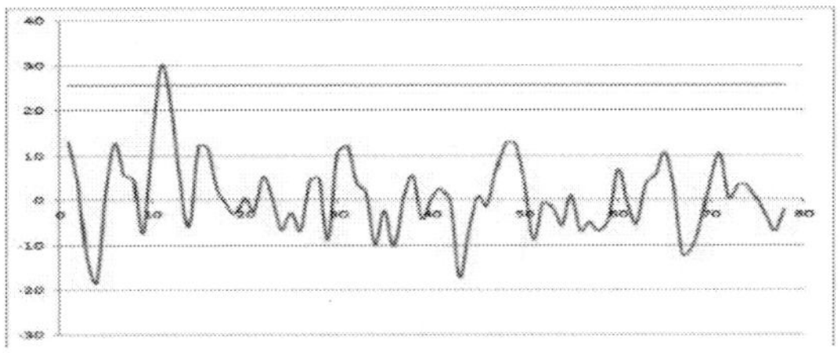

Figure 5. Control chart for residuals of differences of the second order related to measurements of blood pressure with a shifted process level.

control limits. For a "strong" alarm it is necessary to observe at least two consecutive points on the chart situated beyond the control limits.

It has to be stressed here, that the proposed procedures are based on rather heuristic reasoning, based on observations of a particular series of measurements. Unfortunately, closed mathematical formulae that describe statistical properties of a control chart when observed values of measurements are statistically dependent, as for now, do not exist (except for the simplest cases). Therefore, the properties of the proposed procedures have to be investigated in the future using complex simulation experiments.

IV. USING THE sXWAM CONTROL CHART FOR SHORT PROCESS RUNS

One of the most important characteristics of a control chart is its rate of false alarms. An alarm is considered false if it is generated in a period of time when a monitored process is stable. False alarm rate is usually accompanied with good abilities to detect process disorders, so if this falsity does not lead to serious consequences, higher false alarm rates may be considered acceptable. However, when an alarm cannot be neglected because of its serious consequences, the false alarm rate should very low. For example, in certain pharmaceutical production processes an alarm should trigger a stop of a process, and this may be very costly if the triggering alarm is false. In the case of a stable process, described by the model $AR(-0.987, -0.805, -0.217. - 0.133)$ estimated from a sample of $n = 20$ observations, a chart presented in Figure 6 exhibits two false alarms.

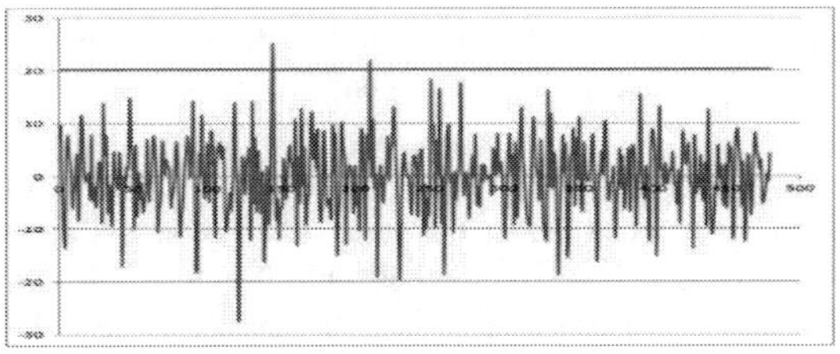

Figure 6. Control chart for residuals with two false alarms.

It has been observed by many authors (see [4], for more information) that control charts for autocorrelated data, especially those designed using small samples of observations, have elevated false alarm rates. Hryniewicz and Kaczmarek-Majer [4] have noted that this rather unfavorable property is somewhat related to the problem of bad predictability in short time series. Inspired by the very good properties of their prediction algorithm for short time series [17], they proposed in [4] a new control chart for residuals, named the XWAM control chart, based on the concept of model averaging.

Let us denote by M_0 the model of a monitored process estimated from a (usually) small sample, and describe its parameters by a vector $(a_{1,0},\ldots.a_{p_0,0})$. We assign to this estimated model a certain weight $w_0 \in [0,1]$. We also consider k alternative models $M_j, j=1,\ldots,k$, each described by a vector of parameters $(a^0_{1,j},\ldots,a^0_{p_j,j})$. In general, any model with known parameters can be used as an alternative one, but in this paper we restrict ourselves to the models chosen according to an extended version of the algorithm described in [11]. Let $w^{'}_1,\ldots,w^{'}_k$ denote the weights assigned to models $M_1,\ldots,M_k$ by this algorithm when only alternative models are considered. Because the total weight of the chosen alternative models is $1-w_0$, to the estimated model we assign the weight w_0, and to each chosen alternative model we will assign a weight $w_j=(1-w_0)w^{'}_j, j=1,\ldots,k$.

When we model our process using $k+1$ models (one estimated from data, and k alternatives) each process observation generates $k+1$ residuals. In the case of differences of the first order considered in this paper, they are calculated using the following formula

$$z_{i,j}=d_i-(a_{1,j}d_{i-1}+\ldots+a_{p_j,j}d_{i-p_j}), j=0,\ldots,k; i=p_j+1,\ldots \quad (8)$$

In (8), we have assumed that for a model with $p_j, j=0,\ldots,k$ parameters we need exactly p_j previous consecutive observations in order to calculate the first residual. Therefore, we need $i_{min}=\max(p_0,\ldots,p_k)+1$ observations for the calculation of all residuals in the sample. For the calculation of the parameters of the XWAM control chart we use $n-i_{min}+1$ weighted residuals calculated from the formula

$$z^\star_i=\sum_{j=0}^{k} w_j z_{i,j}, i=i_{min},\ldots,n. \quad (9)$$

The central line of the chart is calculated as the mean of $z^\star_i$, and the control limits are equal to the mean plus/minus three standard deviations of $z^\star_i$, respectively. The operation of the XWAM control chart is a classical one. First decision is made after i_{min} observations. The weighted residual for the considered observation is calculated according to (9), and compared to the control limits. An alarm is generated when the weighted residual falls beyond the control limits.

The method for the construction of the XWAM chart was firstly proposed by Hryniewicz and Kaczmarek in [4] where they proposed an algorithm for the calculation of the weights of alternative models. This algorithm is based on the methods of computational intelligence, namely the DTW (Dynamic Time Warping) algorithm for comparison of time series. Unfortunately, this algorithm is computationally demanding, so in [11] they proposed its simplification, coined as the sXWAM (simplified XWAM). In this approach, Hryniewicz and Kaczmarek proposed not to compare original time series (observed and alternative), but their summarizations in terms of the autocorrelation functions of the pth order. Let $r_1,r_2,\ldots,r_p$ be the consecutive p values of the sample autocorrelation function, calculated using (2). Similarly, let $r_{1,i}, r(2,i),\ldots,r_{p,i}, i=1,\ldots,J$ be the consecutive p values of the autocorrelation function of an alternative model. For given parameters of the alternative autoregression process $a_{1,i},\ldots,a_{p,i}, i=1,\ldots,J$ the values of $r_{1,i}, r(2,i),\ldots,r_{p,i}, i=1,\ldots,J$ can be found by solving the Yule - Walker equations (3). In general, the consecutive values of r_p can be computed using the following recursion equation

$$r_p=a_1r_{p-1}+a_2r_{p-2}+\cdots+a_p \quad (10)$$

Just like in [11], in this paper we consider only processes of the maximum fourth order. In such a case, explicit formulae for the first three autoregression coefficients are the following [11]:

$$r_1=A_1, \quad (11)$$

$$r_2=a_1A_1+a_2, \quad (12)$$

$$r_3=\frac{a_1B_1+a_3+(a_2+a_4)(A_1+A_2B_1)}{1-a_1B_2-(a_2+a_4)(A_2B_2+A_3)}, \quad (13)$$

where

$$A_1=\frac{a_1}{1-a_2}, \quad (14)$$

$$A_2=\frac{a_3}{1-a_2}, \quad (15)$$

$$A_3=\frac{a_4}{1-a_2}, \quad (16)$$

$$B_1=\frac{A_1(a_1+a_3)+a_2}{1-(a_1+a_3)A_2-a_4}, \quad (17)$$

$$B_2=\frac{A_3(a_1+a_3)}{1-(a_1+a_3)A_2-a_4}. \quad (18)$$

Hence, the consecutive values of $r_4, r_5,\ldots$ can be directly computed from (10).

As the measure of distance between the estimated autocorrelations $r_1,r_2,\ldots,r_p$ and the correlations calculated for the ith alternative model $r_{1,i},r_{2,i},\ldots,r_{p,i}, i=1,\ldots,J$ Hryniewicz and Kaczmarek-Majer [11] used a simple sum of absolute differences (called the Manhattan distance in the community of data mining)

$$dist_{i,MH}=\sum_{k=1}^{p}|r_k-r_{k,i}|, i=1,\ldots,J. \quad (19)$$

In this paper, we consider a slightly more general version of the sXWAM chart. As our alternative models, we consider those autoregression models with k lowest values of $dist_{i,MH}$. Their weights, after some standardization, are inversely proportional to the distances of the closest models. The design of the sXWAM chart for residuals is thus much simpler than the original XWAM chart. The values of the autoregression functions for different alternative models can be computed in advance, and stored in an external file. This file can be read by a computer program, and used for choosing the model that fits to the observed sample (and its estimated autoregression function).

The example of the sXWAM chart is presented in Figure 7 for the same original data that have been used for the construction of the control chart presented in Figure 6. For the design of this chart it was assumed that the weight for sample data is $w_0 = 0.7$. Five alternative process models have been found using the algorithm described above: $AR(-0.9, 0.5, 0.4, -0.3)$ with relative weight $w_1' = 0.201$, $AR(0.8, 0.7, -0.5, -0.3)$ with relative weight $w_2' = 0.201$, $AR(-0.9, 0.5, 0.4, -0.3)$ with relative weight $w_3' = 0.200$, and $AR(-0.8, 0.7, 0.5, -0.3)$ with relative weight $w_4' = 0.199$, and $AR(0.8, 0.5, -0.3, 0.4)$ with relative weight $w_5' = 0.199$. We can see that in this case we have observed only one

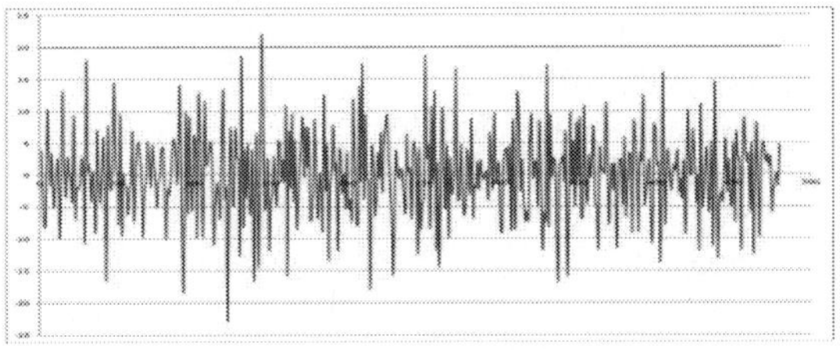

Figure 7. Control chart for weighted residuals with one false alarm.

alarm generated at the same time point as one of the alarms generated on the control chart with non-weighted residuals. Experiments with artificially shifted process levels have shown that the detection ability of the proposed sXWAM chart are similar to that observed for the chart with non-weighted residuals.

V. CONCLUSIONS

In this paper, we have considered monitoring stability of short and non-stationary processes using a simple tool such as a Shewhart control chart. Such processes are typical for health-recovery processes, where natural randomness of measured health-related characteristics is accompanied by random or deterministic trends. Statistical analysis of non-stationary processes is usually very difficult and costly for implementation, as it requires large amount of available data and sophisticated specialized software. It can be used at intensive-care hospital units or in cases when patient's life is endangered. However, in many cases, it is completely sufficient to monitor the state of health using personal measuring devices, and to alarm a patient (or his/hers physician) only in the case of unexpected events. We are of the opinion that this can be done using simple tools, like control charts, by simple software implemented in personal measurement equipments. For this reason we have decided to propose such a chart in this paper.

In our research, we assume that at its initial stage the monitored process is supervised (e.g., by a physician), and considered as stable. Data from this stable period, considered as our sample data, are used for the identification of the monitored process and construction of a control chart. Because simple methods for monitoring non-stationary processes do not exist, we propose to monitor differences of the first order (i.e,, differences between values of consecutive measurements). This approach is effective for linear or approximately linear trends. When we consider, as in this paper, short series of observations, this assumption seems to be rather realistic. However, it is possible to apply the proposed methodology for differences of a higher order. For example, in this paper, we also consider differences of the second order which can be used in the case of processes with alternating (e.g., morning and evening) process levels. In our investigations we have assumed that our series of observations are rather short, and the monitored process has to be identified using a small sample of measurements. This assumption reflects reality when health-recovery processes is evaluated by a physician for only short time, and the period in which the process has to be stable is also short (e.g., until a next treatment is applied). For this reason, we have proposed a novel statistical tool, sXWAM chart, developed recently by us.

The performance of the proposed method has been verified using real-life data. Unfortunately, the amount data, considered in this research, is rather limited, so the presented results should be viewed as a kind of proof of the concept. Further investigations using real and simulated data are needed for more precise evaluation of the statistical properties of the proposed monitoring procedure.

REFERENCES

[1] D. Montgomery, Introduction To Statistical Quality Control, 6th ed. New York: J.Wiley, 2011.

[2] W. Woodall, "The use of control charts in health-care and public-health surveillance," Journal of Quality Technology, vol. 38, no. 2, 2006, pp. 89 – 104.

[3] T. Wiemken et al., "Process control charts in infection prevention: Make it simple to make it happen," American Journal of Infection Control, vol. 45, no. 3, 2017, pp. 216–221.

[4] O. Hryniewicz and K. Kaczmarek-Majer, "Monitoring of short series of dependent observations using a XWAM control chart," in Frontiers in Statistical Quality Control 12, S. Knoth and W. Schmid, Eds. Springer, 2017, p. (in press).

[5] G. Moody and L. Lehman, "Predicting acute hypotensive episodes: The 10th annual physionet/computers in cardiology challenge," Computers in Cardiology, vol. 36, 2009, pp. 541–544.

[6] J. Henriques and T. Rocha, "Prediction of acute hypotensive episodes using neural network multi-models," Computers in Cardiology, vol. 36, 2009, pp. 549–552.

[7] M. Mneimneh and R. Povinelli, "A rule-based approach for the prediction of acute hypotensive episodes," Computers in Cardiology, vol. 36, 2009, pp. 557–560.

[8] F. Chiarugi, "Predicting the occurrence of acute hypotensive episodes: The physionet challenge," Computers in Cardiology, vol. 36, 2009, pp. 621–624.

[9] F. Jousset, M. Lemay, and J. Vesin, "Predicting acute hypotensive episodes," Computers in Cardiology, vol. 36, 2009, pp. 637–640.

[10] D. Jiang, L. Li, B. Hu, and Z. Fan, "An approach for prediction of acute hypotensive episodes via the hilbert-huang transform and multiple genetic programming classifier," International Journal of Distributed Sensor Networks, 2015.

[11] O. Hryniewicz and K. Kaczmarek-Majer, "Monitoring series of dependent observations using the sxwam control chart for residuals," in Soft modelling in industry, ser. Studies in Systems, Decision and Control, P. Grzegorzewski and A. Kochanski, Eds. Springer, 2017, p. (in press).

[12] P. Brockwell and R. Davis, Introduction to Time Series and Forecasting, 2nd ed. New York: Springer, 2002.

[13] G. Box, G. Jenkins, and G. Reinsel, Time Series Analysis. Forecasting and Control. Hoboken NJ: J.Wiley, 2008.

[14] C. Collomb, Burg's Method, Algorithm and Recursion, 2009, [retrieved: April, 2017]. [Online]. Available: http://www.emptyloop.com/technotes/

[15] H. Akaike, "Time series analysis and control through parametric model," in Applied Time Series Analysis, D. Findley, Ed. New York: Academic Press, 1978, pp. 1 – 23.

[16] L. Alwan and H. Roberts, "Time-series modeling for statistical process control," Journal of Business & Economic Statistics, vol. 6, 1988, pp. 87 – 95.

[17] O. Hryniewicz and K. Kaczmarek, "Bayesian analysis of time series using granular computing approach," Applied Soft Computing Journal, vol. 47, 2016, pp. 644–652.

USAMED Learning Object - Usability in Digital Educational Materials for Seniors

Planning, Development and Implementation

Tássia Priscila Fagundes Grande, Leticia Rocha Machado, Ana Luisa Fonseca, Larissa Camargo Justin, Sibele Pedroso Loss, Patricia Alejandra Behar
Federal University of Rio Grande do Sul, Brazil
Avenue Paulo Gama, 110 - Building 12105 - 3rd floor living room 401.
Porto Alegre, Rio Grande do Sul, Brazil
tpri.fagundes@hotmail.com, leticiarmachado@gmail.com, alcfonseca1@gmail.com, larissacjustin@gmail.com, sibeleloss@gmail.com, pbehar@terra.com.br

Abstract— **The aim of this paper is to present the planning, development and implementation of USAMED learning object - Usability in Digital Educational Materials for Seniors. The object was developed in 2015 and has the purpose of discussing how to develop materials for mobile devices following usability guidelines that consider the needs of older people. The USAMED was planned and developed from the methodology suggested by Amante and Morgado (2001): a) Project Design; b) Planning; c) Implementation; d) Evaluation. During the development process, we observed the lack of information about the importance of the design of pre-planning to meet the need for responsiveness of the material and the pedagogical suitability to entice users to use it in practice. It was observed that the USAMED object may help different professionals in the planning and development of Digital Educational Materials (DEM) for seniors who use mobile devices on a day-to-day basis.**

Keywords—learning object; elderly; mobile devices; usability.

I. INTRODUCTION

Every year, digital technologies have been increasingly becoming an integral part of people's daily lives. In recent years, the number of mobile devices being marketed and acquired by the public (such as smartphones and tablets) has significantly increased. A research by the Getúlio Vargas Foundation University [1] of São Paulo indicated that, in 2015, there were 306 million devices connected to the Internet, 154 million of which were smartphones. At the same time, the number of elderly people has increased. According to the data of Brazilian's Institute of Geography and Statistics (IBGE), life expectancy in 2015 was 75.2 years, highlighting that Brazil's population life expectancy has been increasing [1].

Therefore, like younger people, the elderly are also acquiring or receiving mobile devices, especially smartphones, from their family members. However, older people have difficulty in handling such devices, both because of a lack of experience as well as other difficulties that such technologies present to the elderly, like the need for sensibility in the fingers to handle the touch screens, the small size of the screens, and so on. These obstacles can develop frustration and anguish for the elderly public, becoming necessary to develop actions that include them and enable them to use the technologies, in addition to theoretical discussions on possible strategies that can aid the elderly with the use of these resources or even the development of materials by different professionals for these public.

Based on this scenario, many questions arise, specially in the educational field: how to enable digital inclusion for the use of mobile devices by the elderly?; Which pedagogical strategies can be adopted for the use of mobile devices by the elderly?; Are there adequate materials to enable the elderly to learn how to use smartphones and/or tablet devices?; How to develop materials that may suit the older public in the use of mobile devices?

Starting with these questions, it is necessry to think more about possible guidelines for the development of digital educational materials (DEMs) that may be suitable for the elderly regarding the use of mobile devices. DEMs are educational materials composed of digital resources in their elaboration [3]. This type of material is used with the purpose of approaching with the use of technologies, being an advance of the analog material. Some examples of DEMs are websites, web pages and learning objects (LO). Therefore, in this article, the term Learning Object (LO) will be used as a synonym of Digital Educational Material (DEM). The usability of DEMs plays an important role, as it can influence its increasing use by students, instigating and motivating them to become an active participant. Therefore, the development of LOs may be an option to present educational content in a more dynamic and interactive way.

Therefore, this article aims to introduce the planning, development and implementation of the USAMED Learning Object - Usability in Digital Educational Materials for Seniors. The acronym for the learning object was chosen from its full name in Portuguese. The purpose of this object was to present and discuss, with/for different professionals, how to appropriately develop educational materials for the older public, proposing materials, explanatory texts, evaluation forms and activities in the form of challenges. This object was developed in the first semester of 2015 in order to help teachers and professionals from different areas plan and implement educational materials for mobile devices for the elderlypublic.

Next, we will discuss the use of mobile devices by the elderly, followed by the concepts of digital educational materials. After that, the methodology adopted for the development of this material will be presented, culminating with the presentation and implementation of the USAMED's learning object.

II. Education, Aging and Mobile Devices

The constant changes in the world, especially concerning mobile technologies, impact different sectors of society. Some portions of the population are being digitally excluded because of lack of information or lack of training in the use of mobile devices. Thus, education comes as a way to support the elderly in their search for staying current in different areas, such as technology.

According to the survey "TIC Domiciles and Users 2013", 61% of Brazilians with ages 60 or over have a mobile phone device, referring to a sample of 168.3 million people. In 2006, this rate was 18.9%. The main reasons for the increase were the portability, lightness, discretion and size of mobile devices.

As a consequence, questions arise regarding the needs that come with age, especially in the use of mobile technologies: what educational practices to adopt to include the elderly in the use of digital technologies? How to develop educational materials for mobile devices that addresses the needs of the elderly? Therefore, usability issues have been the subject of new studies that also address the role of usability in the development of digital educational materials for mobile devices.

A. *Education and Aging*

According to IBGE data [2], the elderly population has been growing significantly in Brazil. From 2000 to 2016, the growth went from 2.56%, going to 5.61% and to 8.17%. IBGE projects [2] that the senior public will be 13.44% of the country's population by 2030.

The elderly population's growth can be attributed to several factors, such as improvement in Brazilians' quality of life, development of medicines and diseases treatments, as well as the reduction in child mortality and fertility rates [4].

Osório [4] affirms that social and cultural aspects are strongly linked to the process of aging, therefore, this is not restricted only to psychological and physiological factors. Aging "is also seen as an event of changes in attitudes and mentality, resulting from the relationships established between age groups and their living conditions" [4].

A portion of the senior population seeks to adapt to the changes that are happening in society, especially in what refers to technological advancements. They seek to stay autonomous and active within their aging process [4]. However, there are still preconceived ideas that link the elderly to concepts like dependence, illness and little capacity, which can result in distancing of this public from other individuals.

According to gerontology researches, having a social role is essential for the elderly to achieve a promising aging. The quality of life of the elderly is strongly related to active aging, regarding the improvement of their physical, social or mental potential. According to Both and Portella [5], a relevant alternative that serves as support to keep the elderly active are educational interventions that take into account the interests of the target public, and may be through permanent education. Thus, it is opportune that these interventions take place in order to encourage the elderly in the search for knowledge of the aging process, considering their social environment, their experiences and their uncertainties, respecting their personal needs.

The importance of a permanent education is referenced by Doll [6] and Osório [4]. According to the authors, there is no specific age group for learning. According to Zimerman [8] and Pasqualotti [9], it is necessary to instigate the reasoning of the elderly, fomenting the reflection, communication and interactions, intending to soften the effects of aging. In this context, digital technologies are presented as an alternative to assist in the process of self-knowledge of the elderly. Some elderly have already discovered digital technologies and seek to explore them. Therefore, it is important to be aware of which characteristics of this technology and its use, or not, are significant to the elderly.

This public interest in learning how to use new technologies can be associated with the fact that the technology presents itself as an alternative to promote the interaction with other generations. That is, they can maintain an active communication with friends and family, staying socially active [7]. At the same time, Machado [10] mentions that education, together with digital technologies, can offer cognitive maintenance's alternatives to the elderly, good use of free time and more social contact.

Another factor considered important today, besides the fast access to the Internet, is portability. These are some of the attributes of a digital technology called mobile device. This technology has increasingly influenced the senior public to take and use these resources in their daily life, as they simplify communication and the search for information. Such topics will be discussed next.

B. *The Elderly and Mobile Devices*

There are different types of mobile devices, the most popular ones being tablets and smartphones. The elderly are increasingly seeking to stay current about digital technologies and are motivated to learn how to use more economically accessible mobile technologies. In this sense, teaching about the use of these technologies by this public is important. At the same time, accessible materials for mobile devices are needed, both in interface and in educational aspects.

The main characteristics of mobile devices are the mobility and the possibility of connecting to the Internet, boosting the use of these technologies for different means and environments. Customization also makes mobile devices more attractive as it can be organized to meet each individual's personal needs.

Currently, there is a wide variety of applications for different areas, such as leisure: games, movies, books, travel;

for the job: bank transactions, office tools, information on professions; for health: information on sports, with diet and exercise tips; for education and culture: several study materials, knowledge tests and video lessons, among others. The use of applications for communication purposes is one of the most versatile ones, since there are apps with features that go beyond the voice, it can be for text messages, videos, image, music, text files as well as video conferences.

Therefore, all these characteristics from mobile devices end up increasing its use from different people, including the elderly, especially in regards to communication with family and friends.

However, older people who are interested in using these technologies end up having to adjust to the barriers that arise. After all, technologies are not usually projected considering motor and cognitive difficulties that come up with age [11].

Consequently, different studies have been done regarding usability and accessibility in these devices and in the construction of digital educational materials for them, taking into account the different needs of users.

III. DEMS AND THE ELDERLY

As technology advances, society has been through important transformations in all areas, especially in education. The main catalyst for those changes is the insertion of digital technologies into educational institutions. This makes the development of digital educational materials (DEMs) increasingly evident as a possibility to meet the new demands. In this article, the term Learning Object (LO) will be used as synonym of digital educational material (DEM).

DEM is understood to mean "all educational material that incorporates digital resources in its elaboration" [3]. Therefore, DEMs can be considered an evolution of the analogical material, being used with the intention of approaching technologies.

Some examples of DEMs are learning objects (LO), web pages and, with the advent of mobile devices, applications. Applications, also considered digital educational materials, since they are "[...] programs with few features that run on the operational systems created for these mobile devices, they have proprietary license and closed source license and are only available in repositories known as stores [...]" [12].

Learning objects are materials composed of several medias, such as texts, animations, presentations and videos [13][14]. Some of the benefits that justify the use of LOs in the educational context are flexibility, updating ease, customization, interoperability, increasing the value of knowledge, and ultimately indexing and searching [15].

Learning objects developed by institutions and research groups from different fields are available online through repositories, allowing anyone to access their contents. There are also websites and web pages where users can access their content at any time.

When searching for technologies related information, the elderly end up having contact with materials developed in several courses, such as digital inclusion. This public tends to search for information regarding technological resources, such as computers, notebooks and, increasingly, mobile devices. This way, developers of DEMs need to think over and analyze possible ways of designing these materials to understand the specifications of new technologies, such as mobile devices, which is increasing in space among users.

According to Machado [10] the first LOs developed for the senior public was only done in 2013. Before that, there were not even LOs aimed to gerontology and education professionals with adequate contents and considering the needs of this public.

When designing a DEM for the elderly, it is important to look at this audience's specific demands, especially regarding mobile devices, as they have different properties than computers. The main differences between them are screen size, touchscreen, and movements, among others. Therefore, it is necessary to analyze these elements and their peculiarities to the development of DEMs [16].

In this perspective, the usability of DEMs aimed at the elderly is essential for the construction, since it facilitates its use. Usability is quoted by some authors as a point that should be considered in the development of digital materials to mobile devices regarding different needs of the public that use them [11]. Nielsen and Budiu [16] pointed out that web usability issues are for mobile devices, but for the latter they are indispensable.

According to the Brazilian Association of Technical Standards ABNT (NBR ISO 9241 - Ergonomic Requirements for Working with Computer Offices) usability is "[...] defined as the capacity that an interactive system offers its user in a given context of operation, for the accomplishment of tasks, in an effective, efficient and pleasant way ".

According to Preece, Rogers and Sharp [17], "usability is usually considered as the factor that ensures that products are easy to use, efficient and enjoyable from the user's perspective." These authors also highlight usability goals for materials, such as having security, both for fear of use issues and for security of technologies; being efficient and effective. The same authors state that the material should be easy to learn how to use, easy to remember and have good utility. They emphasize that it is important to take into account User Experience issues. Therefore, the evaluation of a material usability is essential in its planning, development and improvement.

Therefore, it is important to think which usability indicators would be significant to the development of mobile devices, taking into consideration the target audience, the material purpose and technology type.

The World Wide Web Consortium - W3C [18] highlights some guidelines for mobile websites, such as simple navigation; short URLs; different mobile devices must be taken into account; one must use Web standards in marking, formatting and making content available; avoid using mapped images, frames, nested tables, and pop-ups; do not measure in pixels or absolute units; avoid text entry; label all form controls appropriately; and avoid the use of pop-up windows that cause certain insecurity and confusion in the elderly.

When it comes to mobile devices, these issues need to be reinforced, as they have some different characteristics, such as having less space for writing and reading, since the main way of entry are practically the human fingers, which requires space for action [16]. The authors also reinforce the importance of avoiding unnecessary information, or, if needed, place it in the background, otherwise it may discourage users.

IV. Methodology

The development of learning objects requires planning, communication and technical, pedagogical and design knowledge. Tarouco et al. [14] point out that, for the construction of objects, it is necessary to consider "both inherent aspects of learning theories and to combine the knowledge of areas such as ergonomics, systems engineering, besides taking into consideration the potentialities and limitations of the technology involved". Therefore, the complexity required for the development of learning objects is evident, as well as the need for an interdisciplinary team to be involved.

For the development of the learning object USAMED - Usability in Digital Educational Materials for Seniors, a specific methodology presented by Amante and Morgado [19] was adopted. These authors point out that "Designing, planning and developing educational applications requires, however, the passage through a set of phases that together determine the quality of the final product" [19].

The steps suggested by Amante and Morgado [19] are: a) Project Conception: what, for whom and in what way is the object to be developed; b) Planning: put into practice the first phase of what was designed, the so-called storyboard-model of what will be created; c) Implementation: all points planned during project development and planning will be put into practice; d) Evaluation: set of evaluated procedures and validation of the product.

Thus, these steps were the base for developing the USAMED object, as detailed next:

Step 1 - Project Design: The project objective was initially outlined, specifying the final user profile, as well as emerging needs to meet the material objectives. The variables responsiveness, usability and accessibility were considered, as well as the user profile diversity.

Step 2 - Planning: After the initial design of the object, the operating storyboard was made, on which the possible links, modules and technological resources that could be used in the object were listed. Also, wireframes of the screens to adjust the screen layout (location of the elements that will compose the interface) were developed. The navigation was readjusted during the process to suit the needs that arose (for example, use of such object in mobile devices and usability to meet this need), as well as accessibility issues.

Step 3 - Implementation: In this step, the planning and design of the storyboard were put into practice. For that matter, a survey was made on possible metaphors that could be adopted for the interface of the object, considering three areas: mobile devices, seniors and usability. A selection of the materials and contents was also made.

Step 4 - Evaluation: For the accomplishment of this step, it was used the evaluation form of usability developed in a master's dissertation work [20]. After analyzing the object, we intend to apply it in an extension course that will be offered at the University in 2018, where the improvement of professionals who wish to develop a DEM for mobile devices for the older public is sought.

It should be noted that the object's team, composed of pedagogues, gerontologists and designers, accomplished all stages. For the planning and development process, bi-weekly meetings were held where the individual and collective tasks of the team members were divided.

This methodology was used because it is the recurrent one for the construction of learning objects in Brazil. The team developed a new methodology called ConstruMED [22]. However, this new methodology was developed after the construction of the object and is based on competencies, the focus not being adopted on the Object.

V. Results

The purpose of USAMEDs - Usability in DEMs for Senior is to discuss and deepen usability issues regarding Digital Educational Materials (DEM) for the elderly, focusing primarily on new frameworks to meet the needs of mobile devices. The object is available in the University's repository (http://www.lume.ufrgs.br/), as well as through the website: http://nuted.ufrgs.br/oa/usamed. The USAMED learning object was developed and published in Portuguese language in Brazil. This LO was developed by an interdisciplinary team of the Nucleus of Digital Technology Applied to Education (NUTED), and has as target audience professionals from different areas: teachers, designers, programmers, gerontologists etc. Therefore, the object can be used as a subsidy to create educational materials on mobile devices aimed at the elderly, with four modules available:

1) DEMs for the elderly: this module deals with the concepts of DEMs, repositories and developed examples specifically for the older public;

2) Usability in DEMs: discussion on what is usability, its theoretical application in digital educational materials and analysis tests;

3) Usability recommendation: here, specific usability parameters for the elderly public are pointed out, responsiveness issues (in order to meet the demand of mobile technologies) and application examples;

4) Online tools: possible digital tools for building DEMs are presented in order to apply usability recommendations to the older audience.

Each module has explanatory texts on the presented subjects, including links to videos, online pages, images, and so on. Support materials built by the team itself in a dynamic way that allows a greater understanding of the issues addressed; Challenges, in the form of activity, that intend to problematize the questions presented during the modules. Some of the texts wording that may be difficult to understand were conceptualized, in order to facilitate the usability and to enable a better understanding of it.

The object also includes, in addition to the modules, a user guide page about the object itself for the user-student, as well as a user guide with possible strategies that the user-teacher can adopt for the use of the objects in their practices. Credits are also available presenting the developer team (both the pedagogical and design group).

For a better understanding, in the next section, we will analyze and point out the results found in the developed object and two categories: Design and Educational Gerontology.

A. Design

The user interaction with the interface can directly influence the learning process, and may or may not motivate the user to continue to explore the material [3]. Thus, a design of easy navigation and exploration was adopted in the LO, not relying on depth or specific knowledge on the computer resources for its manipulation.

The object followed the standards of the World Wide Web Consortium (W3C) accessibility [18]. For usability issues we considered the studies of Nilsen and Budiu [16], mainly the 10 heuristics suggested by the author, which are: 1) Visibility of system status; 2) Link between the system interface and the real world; 3) User freedom and control; 4) Consistency and standards; 4) Error prevention; 5) Recognition rather than recall; 6) Flexibility and efficiency of use; 7) Aesthetics and minimalist design; 8) Support for users to recognize, diagnose and recover from errors; 9) Help and documentation.

In this sense, the interface was thought from its users, professionals from different areas who wish to work with the elderly. In view of the target audience and objectives of the object, it was possible to delimit the general requirements of the interface such as the indispensability of working fully on mobile devices. It was also necessary to exercise caution with users who did not have technical knowledge about digital technologies, considering users' needs and mobile devices' uses. Thus, it was determined the use of a grid on the home page and a simple layout of columns on the internal pages. The grid on the page and the simpler layout on the inside pages make it easier to transition between LO on your mobile device and your computer (Figure 1).

Figure 1. USAMED Responsibility.

After the initial research in which the initial requirements of the users and the objectives of the object were exposed, we set out to generate alternatives that could meet these demands. For such, the brainstorming method was applied first, where the objective was the definition of the main problems and the creation of initial concepts at the beginning of a project. After that, during meetings with the pedagogical team, a sketch of the initial layout concepts based on the content already created was designed. From these sketches, associations of the main layout schemes were created (Figure 2).

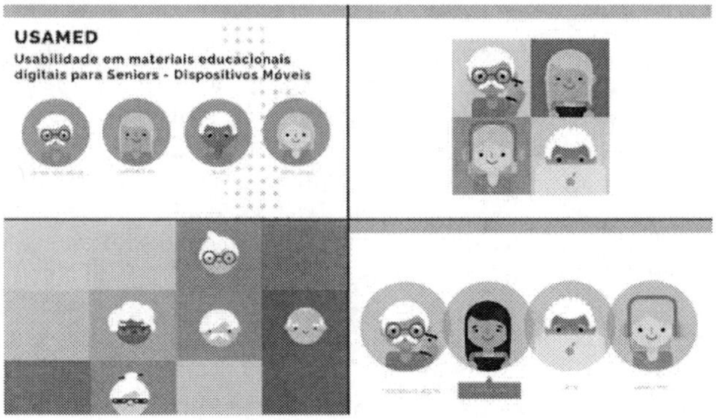

Figure 2. Initial Home Sketches.

Since the object was to aid users who would teach seniors, it was decided to use a color palette that was pleasing to this public. Several texts refer to the use of pastel colors when mentioning the older population, to pass a tranquility and serenity notion. For this reason, less saturated colors and pastels were used in the first schemes. In the next interactions of the color palette, the spectrum has decreased, tending to more monochromatic or analogous situations to exalt the concept of set to all the modules. For the implementation it was decided to use a monochromatic set of blues, tending to the less saturated ones. According to Heller [21] in her book Psychology of Color, blue is the favorite color of 46% of men and 44% of women, being also acknowledged as the color of sympathy, harmony and trust. Pink has been defined to serve as an accent on buttons to add interest and force to the layout.

Because LO is composed mostly of texts, typography serves as an important tool for user comfort. For this project, the use of Roboto font in the text body and Raleway for titles was chosen. Google, developed especially for use on the web and open source nature, meaning that anyone can download, modify and use it for personal or commercial projects, authors both fonts. The fonts are offered in different weights and are available with Portuguese language accents. Font size, line spacing, and kerning were taken into account to ensure readability across devices.

From the definition of the elements previously mentioned, the wireframes of the LO pages were elaborated. The goal of this step is to design a page starting from the structural level. Typically, this method is used at the beginning of projects to establish the basic structure of a page before adding visual design and content. Afterwards, a prototype is produced, where colors and actual content are added before implementation begins. Then, the prototype implementation of the learning object was coded using HTML, CSS and Javascript/Jquery (Figure 3).

Figure 3. USAMED interface.

B. *Educational-Gerontology*

The content of the object was developed to attend to the needs of the elderly who will access educational materials on mobile devices. To meet this proposal, the pedagogical team, composed of undergraduates, graduates and postgraduates in education and/or gerontology, developed contents that can be accessed in the order in which it was presented or randomly, according to the user's needs.

The object also has, as reference, results of studies based on the needs of the elderly in the use of mobile technologies, as well as from experiences in digital inclusion courses [6][7]. In addition to these aspects, the physiological, psychological and cognitive changes of the elderly and their influence on the teaching and learning process were also considered in the construction of the learning object [5].

Explanatory texts: In order to attend to the needs and adapt to mobile devices, the texts of the modules were made in an objective way and with an informal language, in order to approach the user with the approached thematic. The texts were divided into small blocks so that reading on mobile devices is facilitated, and situations and examples that refer to the elderly public were also quoted. Illustrations were used as a complement to the text, in order to instigate the user to read the available material. The references of authors used in the text were listed below it and not in the body, so that there would not be a distruption in the reading. The pedagogical team developed all texts collectively.

Activities: In total, eight challenges were proposed, two on each module. They are presented as activities on which the user can perform in the learning object itself. This could ensure higher autonomy and interactivity in a playful and contextualizing way in the use of LO or combined with other digital resources. In order to achieve this, challenges were proposed that, besides being able to finish out of the object, can also, in some cases, be finished by combining them with a virtual learning reality.

Complementary materials: The materials developed for the object had the purpose of helping the users to deepen their knowledge about the addressed topics. They were all developed by the pedagogical team, using different formats, such as explanatory flowcharts, animations, tables, questionnaires, etc. (Figure 4). These materials may serve as a complement to the text of the modules and may be used separately or in conjunction with the proposed challenges in the object.

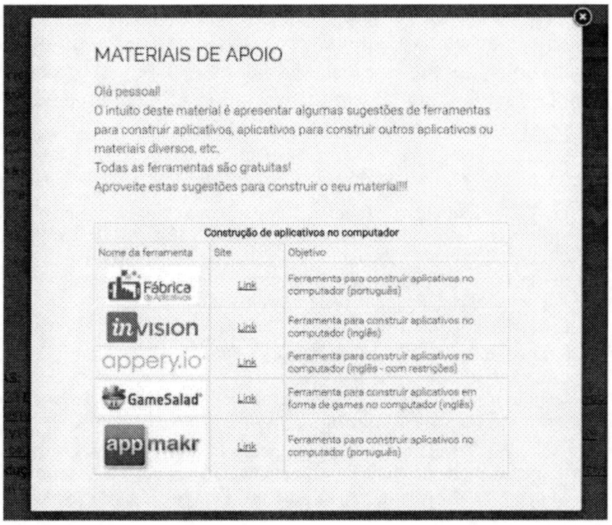

Figure 4. USAMED Tools Module Support Material Interface.

Therefore, from the construction of the modules by the pedagogical team and the layout by the designer, the USAMED learning object became available on the Web. This can be used by anyone who has an interest in it, as well as by using in training and training courses.

VI. FINAL CONSIDERATIONS

The use of mobile devices by the elderly will increase even more in the coming years. Education, as well as other different fields, must be attentive to these changes, discussing and developing materials that can help the older public to handle these technologies. As presented in this article, there is a lot of research being done on usability and mobile devices. However, most of it is focused on the presentation of technologies (screen, layout of applications etc.), with digital education materials being deprived, especially the learning objects. Education has not yet begun a more in-depth reflection on issues concerning the importance and influence of design (usability and accessibility) in DEMS for mobile devices, especially for the elderly public.

Thus, this article's objective was to present the stages of development and implementation of the USAMED learning object that addresses this theme. It is observed that the USAMED object can help different professionals from different fields, such as health, education, technology, etc. in the planning and development of DEMs for seniors who use smartphones and/or tablets on a daily basis.

During the development process, it was possible to observe the lack of information on the importance of design pre-planning to attend to the need for material responsiveness, as well as pedagogical suitability to instigate users to use the object in their practices.

One of the main contributions of the USAMED object is the updated materials on the subject, as well as examples and forms that present usability guidelines that users can use to evaluate their materials constructed or under construction. In this perspective, more research and more in-depth discussions on the subject should take place in order to enable the planning and implementation of new educational materials on mobile devices for the elderly.

VII. References

[1] FGV - Fundação Getúlio Vargas University. "Smartphone number outperforms computers" [26th Annual Information Technology Report. 2015]. Available in: Http://exame.abril.com.br/tecnologia/noticias/numero-desmartphones-supera-o-de-computers-in-brasil

[2] IBGE - Brazilian Institute of Geography and Statistics. "Life expectancy of Brazilians. 2015". Available at: http://g1.globo.com/ciencia-e-saude/noticia/2015/12/expectativa-devida-so-brasileiros-sobe-para-752-anos-diz-ibge.html.

[3] C.A.W Torrezzan. "Pedagogical Design: a look at the construction of digital educational materials". Dissertation, Postgraduate Master in Education. Federal University of Rio Grande do Sul, 2009.

[4] A. R Osório. "The elderly in today's society". In: A. R Osório, F.C. Pinto. The elderly: social context and educational intervention. Lisbon: Instituto Piaget, 2007.

[5] A. Both, R. Portella. "Gerontology: a socio-educational proposal for the elderly". In: A. Both, M.H.S. Barbosa, C.R., Benfica. Human aging: multiple looks. Background: UPF, 2003.

[6] J. Doll. "Education and Aging: fundamentals and perspectives". The third Age, vol. 19, pp. 7-26, n.43, 2008.

[7] J. Doll, L.R. Machado. "The elderly and new technologies". In: E. Freitas, L. Py, F.A. Cançado, J. Doll, M. L. Gorzoni. (Org.). Geriatrics and Gerontology Treaty. Rio de Janeiro: Guanabara Koogan, 2011.

[8] G. I. Zimerman. "Old age: biopsychosocial aspects". Porto Alegre: Artmed, 2000.

[9] A. Pasqualotti. "Development of social aspects in old age: experimentation of computerized environments". In: A. Both et al. Human aging: multiple looks. Background: UPF, 2003.

[10] L. R. Machado. "Construction of a pedagogical architecture for cyberseniors: revealing the inclusive potential of distance education". Dissertation, Postgraduate Master in Education. Federal University of Rio Grande do Sul, 2013..

[11] L. G. N. O. Santos, L. Ishitani, C.N. Nobre. "Use of casual games on mobile phones by the elderly: a usability study". Journal of Applied Informatics, vol. 9, n 1, 2013. Available at <http://www.ria.net.br/index.php/ria/article/view/88>.

[12] B.G.B.Neves, R.S. Melo, A.F. Machado. "Mobile universe: a free educational application for mobile devices". Free Text: Language and Technology, vol.7, 2014.

[13] P.A.Behar et al. "Pedagogical Models in Distance Education". Porto Alegre: Artmed, 2009.

[14] L. Tarouco. "CESTA Project - Collection of Entities to Support the Use of Technologies in Learning". S / ED: Porto Alegre, 2003.

[15] M.F.C Souza et al. "LOCPN: Petri nets. Learning Objects Production". Revista Brasileira de Informática em Educação, vol. 15, pp. 39-42, 2007.

[16] J. Nielsen, R. Budiu. "Mobile usability". Rio de Janeiro: Elsevier, 2014.

[17] J. Precce, Y. Rogers, H. Sharp. "Interaction design: beyond human - computer interaction". Porto Alegre: Bookman, 2005.

[18] W3C - World Wide Web Consortium. "Webdesign for mobile". 2015. Available at: <http://www.w3.org/standards/Webdesign/mobilWeb>.

[19] L. Amante, L. Morgado. "Methodology of design and development of educational applications: the case of hypermedia materials". Discourses, III Series, special issue, pp.125-138, Open University, 2001.

[20] T.P. Grande. "Digital educational materials for the elderly: searching for usability indicators for mobile devices". Dissertation Project in Education. Federal University of Rio Grande do Sul, 2015.

[21] V. Heller. "Psychology of color: How colors act on feelings and reason". Barcelona: Gustavo Gilli SA. 2008.

[22] ConstruMed. Available at: http://nuted.ufrgs.br/oa/construmed/

Medical Sign Language Dictionary with 3D Animation Viewer

Yuji Nagashima
Kogakuin University
2665–1, Makano–machi, Hachioji–shi,
Tokyo, 192–0015, Japan
Email:nagasima@cc.kogakuin.ac.jp

Keiko Watanabe
Kogakuin University
1–24–2, Shinjiku–ku, Tokyo,
163–8677, Japan
Email:ed13001@ns.kogakuin.ac.jp

***Abstract*—This paper reports on the medical sign language dictionary for medical use, which shows the sign language motions in 3D animation. The dictionary includes a viewer function. Because the dictionary contains 3D images of sign language motions that were obtained using motion capture technology, the viewer function enables users to see the sign language motions from any viewpoint they choose. Further, the dictionary also enables words to be searched by hand shape or motion.**

Keywords–Sign Language; Medicine-Clinical Terms; Dictionary; 3D Animation

I. INTRODUCTION

In many cases, sign language native speakers do not seek medical attention until their condition becomes critical. The causes of this problem include the absence of sign language words that are appropriate for expressing their complaints and the absence of appropriate sign language expressions for explaining their medical conditions. However, accurate sign expressions are required in those settings because vital issues may be discussed. Moreover, existing sign language dictionaries have been compiled with the use of pictures, photos and videos. A problem arises in that medical sign language varies considerably in style from one region to another and has not been standardized. In addition, there are currently no dictionaries that allow users to view sign motions based on 3D animation from any viewpoint.

To address this, we are collecting medical words and studying sign language expressions of the words with the aim of unifying and spreading medical sign language expressions [1]. The data of the 3D sign language motions were obtained using optical motion capture technology. The data of the 3D motions are in BVH (BioVision Hierarchy) format. However, we have not yet established a dictionary.

This paper reports on an unprecedented medical sign language dictionary developed by the authors that enables users to view 3D animated images of sign language motions. This dictionary prototypes a model experimentally based on the request of doctors and nurses. In Section II, the dictionary not only contains medical words, but also provides explanations in sign language about medical terms that are believed to be difficult for a sign language native speaker to understand. In Section III, we developed a 3D viewer that renders animated images of sign language in actual time by reading the BVH data. This 3D viewer enables users to check sign language motions as search results by selecting a viewpoint. In Section IV, the dictionary comes with a search function that can be used by entering Japanese words. This function permits free word searches, searches by category, and other types of searches. In addition, regarding searches by sign language element, the dictionary permits searches by hand shape,movement locus of hands, and relationship between left and right hands, among others.

II. WORDS AND EXPLANATIONS

As for the words contained in the dictionary, we selected those that are necessary and frequently used for medical practice in a hospital, excluding dental technical terms. The total number of words in the Japanese index is 1,113. The number of sign language words corresponding to the 1,113 Japanese words is 1,272 because synonyms of different movements exist for some of the Japanese words.

Medical terms include a large number of difficult technical terms. The meanings of many of these words are not clearly understood by ordinary people simply by seeing them. As a result, the dictionary includes explanations of words that are believed to be hard to understand without explanations and those whose meanings are likely to be misunderstood. The explanations are provided using sign language expressions that allow native speaker of sign language to understand the meanings of the words. For example, the dictionary includes explanations of diseases such as toxoplasmosis and Kawasaki disease, the meanings of words such as remission, and differences in meaning between virus and bacterium and other pairs of words that are confusing to the general public. A total of 122 explanations are provided about 141 words, with some of them explaining multiple relevant words.

III. 3D VIEWER

The data of the 3D sign language motions were obtained using optical motion capture technology. The data of the 3D motions are in BVH format. We developed a 3D viewer that renders animated images of sign language in actual time by reading the BVH data.

The 3D viewer developed enables users to check the sign language motions of the avatar in a selected direction or from a selected viewpoint in the 3D space. The control panel on the right side of Figure 1 permits the adjustment of the viewpoint (camera position), to zoom in/out, move the image parallel, and rotate it.

IV. SEARCH FUNCTION

The dictionary comes with a search function that permits two types of searches: search by Japanese keyword and search by description of sign language. The search results can be checked by viewing animated images of the sign language using the 3D viewer mentioned in Section III.

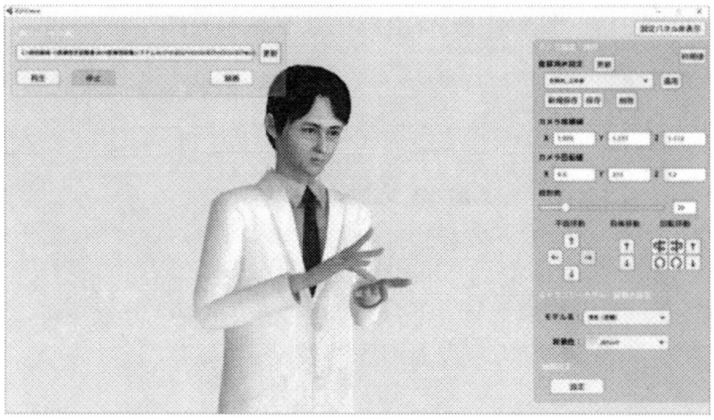

Figure 1. Example of the 3D viewer's screen

A. Search by keyword in Japanese

1) Search of the list of words and explanations: A list of headings in the dictionary is displayed for the search.
2) Search of kanji and hiragana: Search by entering headings consisting of both kanji and hiragana (partial match).
3) Search by hiragana characters for the word: Search by entering hiragana characters for the word (partial match).
4) Search by category: The words contained in the dictionary are classified into 20 categories, including diagnosis and treatment department, name of disease, symptom, and body part, with some of them classified into multiple categories. The dictionary permits searches of the list of words in each category (Table I).
5) Search by keyword used in explanation.

TABLE I. MEDICAL WORD CLASSIFICATION AND EXAMPLE WORDS

Classification	Example words
Parts of body	head, eyelid, foot
Internal organs	neurohypophyis, hormone
Care	full nursing, nursing certification
Facilities	germfree room, ICU (Intensive Care Unit), blood sampling room
Food	grapefruit, natto, alcohol
Hospital departments	internal medicine, pediatric clinic
State	critical condition, remission, climacteric
Medical examination	respiration, heart sound, second opinion
Medicine	tablet, antibiotic, anticancer drug
Name of Diseases	gastritis, Alzheimer's disease, atopic dermatitis
Occupation	medical doctor, nurse, dietician
tests and Tools	medical check-up, blood test, gastrocamera
Secretion	blood serum, cerumen, cerumen
Sports	rugby, sky, malathon, mountaineering
Operation	laparoscopic surgery, suture, anesthesia
Symptom	vomiting, hyperpnea, compression fracture
Treatment	hemostasis, laser treatment, oxygen inhalation
Therapy and rehabilitation	speech therapy, dietary care, palliative care
Receptions	accounting, medical certificate, reservation
otheres	survival rate, traffic accident, QOL (Quality Of Life)

B. Search by symbol describing sign language word

The words contained in the dictionary are described using the NVSG (Nominal Verbal Sightline Grammatical) element model that was suggested by the authors [2]. This method describes morphemes in sign language by dividing each morpheme into hand shape, motion, expression, and gaze. Accordingly, the dictionary permits searches of sign language motions with unknown meanings by hand shape using N element (Figure 2), motion, and other elements.

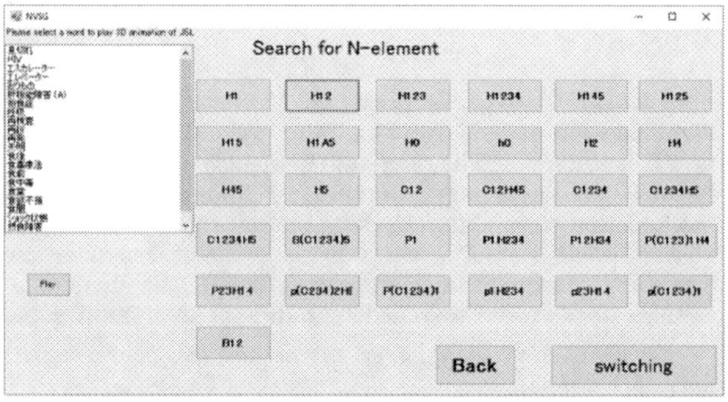

Figure 2. Search screen by the hand shapes

V. CONCLUSION AND FUTURE WORKS

This paper has described the medical sign language dictionary for medical use, which shows the sign language motions in 3D animation. We developed a 3D viewer that renders animated images of sign language in actual time by reading the BVH data. This 3D viewer enables users to check sign language motions as search results by selecting a viewpoint.

As a result, it is possible to use the dictionary as a reverse dictionary in which the meanings of sign language are able to be searched from the shapes and motions of the hands. Moreover, because 3D motion data and the morpheme time structure are linked to each other one by one in the database, it is possible to view sign language based on the morphemes. There have been no sign language dictionaries available with these functions before. The usability and practicality of the dictionary are extremely high. We are getting impression of expressing sign language which can be understood intuitively from medical staff.

We are proceeding with a further study on how to synthesize new words that are not found in the current dictionary by taking advantage of this morpheme dictionary described using NVSG elements. Furthermore, we have to perform a user evaluation in the medical scene of this dictionary.

ACKNOWLEDGMENT

Part of this work was supported by Grants-in-Aid for Scientific Research Grant Number 26244021.

REFERENCES

[1] M. Terauchi and Y. Nagashima , "Study of Sign Language Expression of Medical Sign Language Words," Proc. of the the Ninth International Conference on Advances in Computer-Human Interactions (ACHI 2016), April 2016, pp. 297–298.

[2] K. Watanabe et al. , "Study into Methods of Describing Japanese Sign Language," Proc. of the Communications in Computer and Information Science (CCIS) series, June 2014, pp. 270–275: , HCI International 2014, ISBN: 978-3-319-07853-3.

Evaluation of Gaze-Depth Prediction Using Support Vector Machines

Choonsung Shin, Youmgmin Kim, Jisoo Hong,
Sung-Hee Hong, Hoonjong Kang
VR/AR Research Center
Korea Electronics Technologies Institute
Seoul, Republic of Korea
e-mail:{cshin, rainmaker, jhong, shhong, hoonjongkang}
@keti.re.kr

Youngho Lee
UVR Lab
Dept. of Computer Engineering
Mokpo National University
Jeonnam, Republic of Korea
e-mail: youngho@mokpo.ac.kr

Abstract—**This paper presents the evaluation results of a gaze-depth prediction method for natural gaze interaction of wearable augmented reality. To calculate the gaze depth, we extracted the position of the center of the eyeball and the gaze vector of participants' eyes from a binocular eye tracker while the distance between participants' eyes and an object changed. We then applied support vector machines (SVM) to predict gaze depth. Based on our evaluation, prediction of gaze depth to actual focal distance was accurate to within +/- 20 cm.**

Keywords-gaze depth; eye tracking; augmented reality.

I. INTRODUCTION

Recently, augmented reality (AR) has received great attention from researchers and consumers due to the release of commercial devices from global companies. Smartphones are now commonly used in conjunction with AR SDKs (Software Development Kit), such as Vuforia and Kudan, thus developers easily make AR apps for them [1][2]. Furthermore, AR head-mounted displays (HMDs), such as Hololens have had a big impact on the possibility of AR for consumer business [3].

There have been many studies on improving interaction for AR glasses [4][5]. Researchers have integrated various interaction methods such as hand gesture interaction and gaze tracking for remote collaboration. However, it is still difficult to use hand gesture and control gaze direction. Moreover, Toyama et al. studied multi-focus estimation based on support vector regression for optical see-through HMDs [6]. However, depth estimation has still largely deviated from a user's focal length and thus has caused unstable user interaction.

In this paper, we present the evaluation results of gaze-depth estimation using support vector machines (SVM) based on a binocular tracker. We collected eye vectors and eye centers of both eyes. The collected data was analyzed and used for predicting eye-gaze depth using support vector regression (SVR) an SVM. The learned model was then used to analyze the accuracy of the prediction results.

This paper is organized as follows. In Section II, we first describe the prediction procedure and approach. We then introduce the evaluation result of the prediction approach in Section III. Finally we conclude with future work in Section IV.

II. PREDICTION OF EYE-GAZE DEPTH

Several studies have reported on estimations of gaze depth, and they have shown two categories [6]. One involves the use of 3D eye measurements geometrically based on vector intersection, and the other uses the SVR model. The vector intersection approach calculates eye depth by intersecting the eye vectors of the two eyes. However, the depth information from this method is inaccurate due to the unstable convergence of the human eye. The SVR approach uses a support vector machine that estimates the gaze depth by maximizing the margins of the support vectors. However, this regression still has a large estimation error due to the inherent problems of human eye convergence.

To predict gaze depth in a stable manner, the gaze-depth predicting method uses a binocular tracking device. The binocular eye tracker provides the eye position and eye line information of both eyes. Our research uses the position of the center of the eyeball and gaze information in order to predict eye gaze depth. We thus integrated smart eyeglasses and an eye tracker, as shown on the right side of Figure 1.

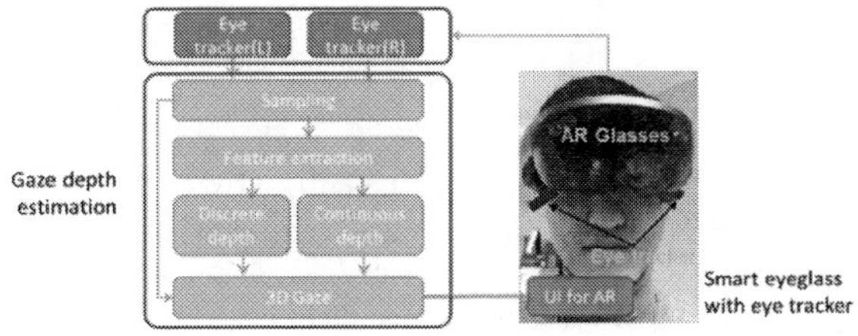

Figure 1. Gaze-depth prediction procedure for wearable 3D interaction

Using this equipment, we collected raw data from the eye tracker to predict eye depth as shown on the left of Figure 1. First, we extracted eye tracker information from the eyes of three test participants and selected features to obtain the gaze depth. Eye movement information includes the pupil position of each eye. Multiple pieces of eye information from the eyes were also collected. From this information, we analyzed and extracted the influential features for eye-depth prediction. Finally, the proposed method estimated the continuous line depth based on the SVR model and predicted the discrete line depth based on the SVM. The support vector model estimated the eye depth based on the maximum margin of the given sample data. With this model, we trained and tested specimens with eye and depth information.

III. EVALUATION

To evaluate the accuracy of gaze depth in the distance, we installed a test bed consisting of a Pupil Labs binocular eye tracker [7]. This eye tracker has two eye cameras and one world camera. It tracks the eye movement and estimates gaze information of each eye and records world image frames at 120 Hz. We collected pupil and gaze data at focal distances of 1, 2, 3, 4, and 5 meters. There was a small panel located at each of the focal distances, and each user was asked to look at each panel. Three participants were involved in this experiment.

We first analyzed influential features for predicting eye-gaze depth. For this purpose, we calculated the importance information gain of each feature with respect to gaze depth. As seen in Figure 2, among the 17 features analyzed, the position of the center of the eyeball is the feature most highly related to eye-gaze depth. The direction of each eye's gaze is also related to eye-gaze depth.

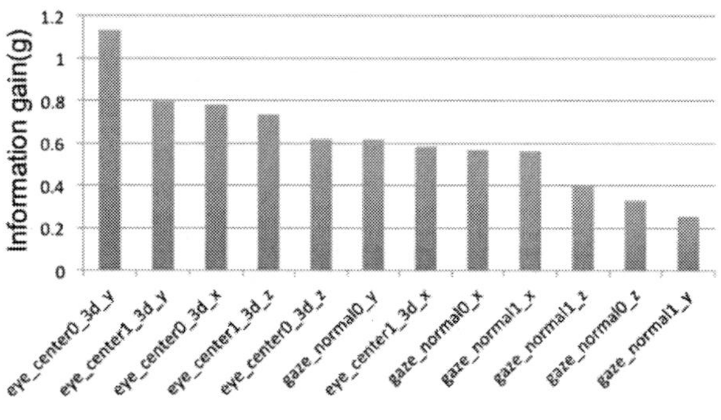

Figure 2. Information gained from features on gaze depth

We then analyzed the performance of continuous gaze-depth prediction obtained from the SVR model. Figure 3 illustrates the relationship between the actual and the predicted gaze depth. The model's prediction of gaze depth to actual focal distance was accurate to within +/- 20 cm (absolute mean error) except for the 2-meter distance.

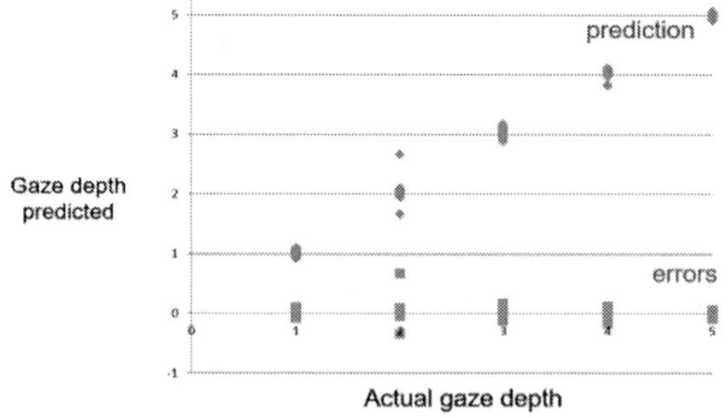

Figure 3. Gaze-depth estimation using the SVR model

Lastly, we evaluated the performance of prediction of discrete gaze depth obtained from the SVM. The overall prediction accuracy was 99% in classifying focal depth. As seen in Table 1, the gaze depths were well classified based on the focal distance. There was only an error in predicting the gaze depth at 4 meters. This indicates that the depth can be predicted by machine learning and discrete prediction might be practically useful for user interaction. However, the results should be tested with a greater number of participants, since only a small number of participants were involved.

TABLE I. CONFUSION MATRIX OF DEPTH CLASSIFICATION FROM SVM

Gaze depth	1	2	3	4	5
1	5971	0	0	0	0
2	0	5874	0	0	0
3	0	0	6415	0	0
4	0	0	0	6109	1
5	0	0	0	0	6449

IV. CONCLUSION

In this paper, we presented the results of the evaluation of gaze depth using a supporting vector machine for natural interaction of wearable AR systems. We set up smart eyeglasses with a binocular eye tracker and then collected pupil and gaze data from the eye tracker. We then evaluated the performance of the gaze-depth prediction based on SVMs.

This work is the first step towards supporting natural gaze interaction based on eye-gaze information for wearable computers. There are still technical problems that need to be improved. We first would like to find features that are more influential in estimating gaze-depth information. We would also like to find more stable and accurate estimation methods for predicting gaze-depth information.

ACKNOWLEDGMENT

This work was supported by the Ministry of Science, ICT and Future Planning (Cross-Ministry Giga Korea Project).

REFERENCES

[1] Vuforia. https://vuforia.com (access date: 2017 Feb. 24)

[2] Kudan. https://www.kudan.eu (access date: 2017 Feb. 24)

[3] Hololens. https://www.microsoft.com/microsoft-hololens/en-us (access date: 2017 Feb. 24)

[4] Y. Lee, K. Masai, K. Kunze, M. Sugimoto and M. Billinghurst, "A Remote Collaboration System with Empathy Glasses," *(ISMAR-Adjunct)*, 2016, pp. 342-343.

[5] M. Billinghurst et al., "Is It in Your Eyes? Explorations in Using Gaze Cues for Remote Collaboration," Collaboration Meets Interactive Spaces, pp.177-199, 2016.

[6] T. Toyama, J. Orlosky, D. Sonntag, and K. Kiyokawa, "A natural interface for multi-focal plane head mounted displays using 3D gaze," In *Proceedings of the 2014 International Working Conference on Advanced Visual Interfaces* (AVI '14). USA, 25-32.

[7] M. Kassner, W. Patera, and A. Bulling, "Pupil: an open source platform for pervasive eye tracking and mobile gaze-based interaction," UbiComp Adjunct, pp. 1151-1160, 2014.

Text Location Algorithm Based on Graph-Cut Model with Unary and Binary Features

Fengqin Yu[1] , Yaya Liu[2]
School of Internet of Things Engineering, Jiangnan University, Wuxi, China
1: e-mail: yufq@jiangnan.edu.cn; 2: e-mail: 8489672@163.com

***Abstract*—In this paper, we propose a location algorithm of the text regions in an image based on a graph cut model with unary and binary features. First, the most stable extremal regions are detected as candidate regions. Then, we define the energy function using unary and binary features of the candidate regions. The text classification is obtained by the optimal segmentation. Lastly, the final positioning is obtained using text aggregation. The simulation results show that the proposed algorithm is better than several classic algorithms in terms of precision rate and standard measurement and can precisely locate text regions in an image.**

Keywords- text location; graph-cut model; unary text features; binary text features.

I. INTRODUCTION

Nowadays, images have become an important carrier of information, while the text embedded in images provides semantic information. Text localization is the positioning of the text area in an image and has become an important research topic in image interpretation and pattern recognition. Text location methods can be divided into three main kinds, namely: edge-based [1]-[2], connected-component-based [3]-[5] and texture-based [6]-[8].

We propose a text location algorithm based on the multi-feature graph-cut model described in Pan *et al.* [3]. First, candidate text regions are identified from the Maximally Stable Extremal Regions (MSER) in a contrast-enhanced input image. Each candidate region is treated as a vertex in the graph-cut model. We define an energy function containing a regional term and a boundary term based on the unary features and the binary features of the candidate regions. Subsequently, the energy function is minimized to classify the candidate text regions and remove the background. Finally, we connect adjacent text regions (text aggregation) and quantify their locations.

The rest of the paper is structured as follows. In Section 2, we present the graph-cut model with unary and binary features. In Section 3, we outline the algorithm implementation steps. Section 4 presents the simulation experiment and results analysis. We conclude the paper in Section 5.

II. GRAGH-CUT MODEL WITH UNARY AND BINARY FEATURES

A. Gragh-Cut Model

The graph-cut model provides a means of image segmentation by mapping an image into a weighted graph, where a chosen pixel in the original image represents the vertex of the graph and the relation between this pixel and the domain translates into the edge of the graph. The energy function is formed with the edge weights, and a solution that minimizes the energy function represents an optimal way of partitioning the given image into text regions and non-text regions (background).

In the graph-cut model, the pixels of the input image correspond to the vertices in the output graph one to one. Every edge has a weight. According to the edge weights, the energy function is formulated as follows:

$$E(L)=\sum_{p\in V}R_p(l_p)+\lambda\sum_{\{p,q\}\in E}B_{\{p,q\}}*\delta(l_p,l_q) \tag{1}$$

where, $L=(l_1,l_2,...l_n)$ are two value vectors, n is the number of vertices, L is the label vector of the graph, and each label vector corresponds to the cut set of an image. V and E are the set of vertices and edges, respectively. p and q are regions. $\sum_{p\in V}R_p(l_p)$ is the region term, $\sum_{\{p,q\}\in N}B_{\{p,q\}}$ is the boundary term, λ is the weight factor, and $\delta(l_p,l_q)$ is the Dirac function.

B. Unary text feature

A unary text feature describes the characteristic of the text region–basically its probability of being text, as opposed to being background. The unary text feature constitutes the regional term in the energy function. The method by Pan *et al.* [3] cannot comprehensively represent text characteristics because it employs only prior characteristic rules, such as standard width and height, aspect ratio, and occupancy. In comparison, our unary text feature includes the edge gradient, center surround histogram, and stroke width coefficient of variation.

C. Binary text feature

A binary text feature describes the relationship between a region of concern and its neighborhood. It reflects the probability of the two regions being the same or different types. The more similar the features of the two regions are, the higher the probability that the two regions are of the same type. The binary text feature constitutes the boundary term in the energy function. Pan *et al.* [3] include only the regional features as the binary text feature; whereas, we consider color images, where the color distribution and the regional similarity are included as binary text features. Two regions p and q, are considered as being adjacent if they satisfy the following criterion:

$$dis(p,q) < 2\times\min\left[\max\left(w_p,h_p\right),\max(w_q+h_q)\right] \quad (2)$$

where, w and h are the width and height of the region and $dis(p,q)$ is the Euclidean distance between the centroids of the two regions p and q.

D. Energy function with Unary and Binary Features

The regional term of the energy function is the sum of the edge weights, and the edge is defined as the link between the vertex and the endpoint; it reflects the regional characteristic. Since the unary text features, edge gradient, center surround histogram, and stroke width coefficient of variation well describe the regional characteristic, we use these features to establish the regional term for the region p .

III. ALGORITHM IMPLEMENTATION STEPS

Step1. The contrast of the input image is enhanced and the MSERs are detected as candidate text regions. The input image is divided into a light-dark image via contrast enhancement.

Step2. Candidate text regions are filtered based on heuristic rules. Each region is treated as a vertex, and a graph model is constructed.

Step3. The regional term of the energy function is formulated from the unary text features, the edge gradient, the center surround histogram, and the stroke width coefficient of variation of the candidate regions.

Step4. The boundary term of the energy function is formulated from the binary text features, the color distribution, and the regional similarity extracted from the candidate regions.

Step5. An optimal segmentation of the candidate regions is obtained by minimizing the energy function, with a weighting factor λ=0.5. The fore-ground are text regions and the rest are removed.

Step6. Adjacent characters are connected based on text aggregation. The bright-dark text image is combined with the original image to produce the final text positioning result.

IV. SIMULATION EXPERIMENT AND RESULTS ANALYSIS

In order to test and verify the validity of our algorithm in segmenting and labeling text regions, we employed the dataset publicly available from International Conference on Document Analysis and Recognition (ICDAR), which is composed mainly of various indoor and outdoor images taken with a digital camera.

TABLE I. PERFORMANCE COMPARISON

Method	Precision Rate	Recall rate	Standard Measure
Proposed Algorithm	0.75	0.68	0.72
Pan [3]	0.67	0.70	0.69
Rodrige [7]	0.74	0.63	0.68
Yi [4]	0.71	0,62	0.67
Epstein [2]	0.73	0.60	0.66

Table 1 compares the performance of the proposed algorithm against several classic algorithms. Compared with [2][3][4][7], the precision rate and the standard measure of the proposed algorithm increased, but the recall rate decreased.

Figure 1. Some location results

As demonstrated in Figure 1, the proposed algorithm successfully isolated text regions from complex backgrounds in various test natural scene images.

V. CONCLUSION

We propose a text localization algorithm that is based on the multi-feature graph-cut model and achieves text classification through optimal segmentation. First, the MSERs are extracted as candidate text regions. Subsequently, each region is treated as a vertex and the graph-cut model is established. An energy function with the regional and boundary terms is constructed from the unary and binary text features, and candidate regions are classified by minimizing the energy function. Finally, adjacent characters are connected together based on text aggregation. We demonstrate that the proposed algorithm is able to locate precisely text regions in a variety of natural scene images.

REFERENCES

[1] B. Epshtein, E. Ofek,and Y. Wexler, "Detecting text in natural scenes with stroke width transform, "Proceedings of the IEEE Computer Society Conference on Computer Vision and Pattern Recognition, pp.2963-2970, 2010.

[2] Z. Zhou and C. L. Tan, "Edge based binarization for video text images. "Proceeding of 20th International Conference on Pattern Recognition. Istanbul,Turkey, pp.133-136,2010.

[3] Y. Pan, X. Hou, and C. Liu,"A hybrid approach to detect and localize texts in natural scene images," IEEE Trans.on Image Processing, vol. 20, pp.800-813, 2011.

[4] C. C. Yi and Y. L. Tian, "Text string detection from natural scenes by structure-based partition and grouping,"IEEE Trans.on Image Processing, vol. 20, pp. 2594-2605, 2011.

[5] X.Yin, K. Huang, and H. Hao, "Robust text detection in natural scene images,"IEEE Trans.on Pattern Analysis and Machine Intelligence, vol.36, pp.70–983,2013.

[6] J.Ye, L. L. Huang, and X. L. Hao, "Neural network based text detection in videos using local binary patterns,"IEEE Chinese Conference on Pattern Recognition(CCPR), pp.1-5, 2009

[7] R.Minetto, N. Thome, and M. Cord, "SnooperText: A text detection system for automatic indexing of urban scenes," Computer Vision and Image Understanding, Vol.122, pp.92-104, 2014.

[8] S.Kumar, R. Gupta, and N.Khanna, "Text extraction and document image segmentation using matched wavelets and MRF model," IEEE Trans.on Image Processing, Vol. 16, pp. 2117-2128, 2007.

Workload Adaptive I/O Fairness Scheme for Modern Cloud Storage

KiSung Jin, SangMin Lee, HongYeon Kim, YoungKyun Kim
Department of High Performance Computing Research, SW contents Laboratory
Electronics and Telecommunications Research Institute
Daejeon, Korea
e-mail: {ksjin, sanglee, kimhy, kimyoung}@etri.re.kr

Abstract—**Although many cloud services have introduced several algorithms for providing Quality of Service (QoS) satisfaction to users, the performance interference problem among services has not yet been solved. Because multiple heterogeneous services produce non-deterministic workloads in the real world, service providers often experience contradictory results in their quality prediction. To solve this phenomenon, we specifically focus on the storage layer among the entire cloud stack. In this paper, we propose a workload adaptive Input/Output (I/O) fairness scheme to guarantee balanced data access regardless of various service workloads. Furthermore, we validate our idea through performance evaluations and show that our algorithm can satisfy QoS requirements in the cloud service.**

Keywords-Cloud; Cloud Storage; I/O Fairness; QoS

I. Introduction

The cloud platform provides large pools of computations and storage resources to heterogeneous services on demand. An increasing number of services are already moving their workloads to cloud platforms. Many of commercial or open platforms, such as Azure [1], Amazon [2], Hadoop [3], Openstack [4] and Cloudstack [5] represent the beginning of a much larger trend. For example, Amazon's Elastic Compute Cloud (EC2) provides practically infinite resources to anyone willing to pay. Following this trend, Gartner estimated that the annual growth rate of cloud services will reach about 16% by 2018 [6].

However, most existing systems still provide weak performance isolation or simple fairness control techniques among multiple services. High-demand or misbehaving services can overload shared resources as well as can disrupt other well planned services. In particular, if one of services gives rise to massive I/O workloads unexpectedly, the remaining services will suffer from poor service quality due to bottlenecks. Such a performance violation implies that paying for quantity of resources does not necessarily mean the user will receive the desired QoS level. This is a key problem, which prevents more services to move to the cloud platform.

By carefully observing this performance violation problem in the cloud platform, we find that the key reason for the poor service quality is mainly due to the I/O interference on the shared storage. Many researches have been still trying to find their solutions in upper layers, such as the application, the server, and the network. However, this approach is regarded as an easy and simple way, but other serious problems still remain. For example, lots of developers can easily add some QoS optimizations to the application layer. In the start-up phase, these approaches may give service providers an illusion that they can control. However, as an increasing number of services are gradually producing data explosions and storage bottlenecks, they would realize that the cloud platform finally reaches a limit that they cannot control. Even if the server and the network layer provide us resource isolation methods with virtualization, they cannot avoid I/O interference problems on the storage.

In this paper, we propose a workload adaptive I/O fairness scheme that controls access fairness among all heterogeneous services sharing the cloud storage. Our algorithm continuously collects workload status from all services, and automatically controls each access ratio to guarantee the I/O fairness. It always guarantees balanced I/O performance regardless of various service workloads. Our model is meaningful in that the quality of service is guaranteed on storage level rather than upper layers, such as the application, the server, and the network. While traditional approaches on upper layers continuously require resource reconfiguration or service optimizations, our model can always assure the QoS among all services based on real I/O workloads.

This paper starts with an overview of QoS problems on the traditional cloud platform in Section 2. Then, we present our proposed model and algorithms to guarantee the quality of service for multiple heterogeneous services in Section 3. In Section 4, we show the superiority of our algorithms through performance evaluation and continue with conclusions in Section 5.

II. Related Works

Recently, there are lots of heterogeneous applications simultaneously working in the cloud platform. Under this environment, because all services try to use the system resources in the best-effort manner, inevitable performance violations can severely degrade the service quality. If one of services overuses the system resources, the remaining services may suffer from the relatively poor performance. Although many researches try to solve this problem, it is very hard to find complete solutions yet. To find the fundamental reason of this problem, we review current activities followed by commonly used cloud architecture.

TABLE I. COMPARISONS OF CURRENT QOS APPROACHES IN CLOUD LAYERS

	Application	Server	Network	Storage
Isolation Object	Service level Bandwidth	Computing Resource	Communication Resource	Physical Storage Device
Isolation Method	Service Optimization	Server Virtualization	Network Virtualization	Partitioning Storage Device
Avoiding I/O Interference	Difficult	Difficult	Difficult	Easy
Continuous Optimization	High	High	Middle	Middle
Technical Maturity	High	High	High	Low

In the SNIA [7], the cloud environment consists of 4 layers: the application, the server, the network, and the storage. We analyzed the role of each layer, as well as the techniques for ensuring QoS at each layer.

Application Layer provides a service logic to end users. Under the scalability feature of the cloud platform, a service provider can add a new service to the application layer at any time. Traditionally, many major cloud computing vendors, such as Amazon [2], Windows Azure [1], Google App Engine [8] provide "pay-per-use fixed pricing" or "pay for resources" model. While they guarantee the minimum rates of the user contract, they do not provide system wide fairness because they assume uniform load distributions across tenant partitions. Hadoop [3] supports resource management scheme for MapReduce framework running on Hadoop Distributed File System (HDFS). It is designed to run Hadoop applications as a shared, multi-tenant cluster in an operator-friendly manner while maximizing the throughput and the utilization of the cluster. Choosy [9] provides Constraint Max-Min Fairness (CMMF) by generalizing previous max-min fairness scheme to handle hard task placement constraints. However, an unpredicted workload pattern caused by multiple heterogeneous applications often confuses the service provider. Even if the service provider can estimate the individual service workload, the interference among multiple services can degrade the overall service qualities.

Server Layer provides computing platforms to applications. In this layer, a recent trend is to use a server virtualization technique, which encapsulates workloads in virtual machines (VMs) and consolidates them on multicore servers. In order to maximize the resource utilization of shared resources, hardware extensions such as caches have been considered extensively in previous work. For example, hardware based control schemes have been proposed dynamically partition cache resources based upon utility metrics [10] or integrate novel data control policies to pseudo-partition caches [11]. Even though resources are sliced and allocated to different VMs, they are still shared and interfere with each other without constraints. The isolation across VMs provided by hypervisors rather amplifies the performance issues demonstrated by several works [12] [13] [14].

Network Layer provides communications between each layer. Recently, as the cloud service is emerging, the virtual private network (VPN) is becoming an important factor for service providers. VPN provides customers with predictable and secure network connections over a shared network. Because the network is essential to organize distributed computing, many optimization techniques have been introduced for a long time. Hose model [15] allows for greater flexibility since it permits traffic to and from an endpoint to be arbitrarily distributed to other endpoints. VMware provides the vNetwork Distributed Switch that combines all virtual switches into one logical centrally managed unit. As an open software cloud platform, OpenStack [4] and CloudStack [5] add the virtual network functionality into their software stack. However, the network virtualization still cannot solve the storage interference problem caused by multiple applications. Even if we configure the well planned network topology, it cannot avoid the storage bottleneck.

Storage Layer manages storing data produced by applications. The storage layer faces different challenges than sharing resources at upper layers. Rather than managing individual storage partitions, the storage layer wants to treat the entire storage system as a single black box. All of the applications share their data on the virtualized storage. While many studies provide differentiated service to workloads accessing a single storage array, their techniques are not suitable for cloud storage but rather a centralized one [16]. Pisces [17] provides per-tenant performance isolation and fairness in shared key-value storage. A server-side I/O coordination scheme is introduced in [18]. However, although some algorithms and models are trying to satisfy storage level QoS for a quite long time, it is relatively hard to find practical solutions comparing to other layer in the cloud.

In Table 1, we summarize the status of current approaches from the perspective of the global QoS control in the cloud service. According to our observations, even if most of cloud layers do their best to control the QoS in their own way, they still cannot avoid I/O interferences caused by multiple simultaneous workloads. Furthermore, they still have an unavoidable side effect, which requires continuous optimizations whenever the service scale or the I/O workload is changed.

III. WORKLOAD ADAPTIVE I/O FAIRNESS SCHEME

To overcome the problems described in Section 1 and Section 2, we propose a purely storage oriented QoS model called the Global QoS algorithm. It always guarantees balanced I/O performance regardless of service workloads. For example, let us suppose there are different types of services running on the storage. If one of the services instantaneously produces unpredicted bursty workloads, it will require to consume more storage bandwidth. Because resources are limited on given hardware configuration, the rest of the services will suffer from the lack of resources. This can degrade overall service qualities and can lead to the unfairness problem among services. Our scheme automatically controls each access ratio to guarantee the I/O fairness.

A. System Architecture

In this section, we suppose a cloud storage architecture composed of three types of nodes; a storage node, a controller node, and a client node, as shown in Figure 1. The storage node is responsible for storing and retrieving the data produced by all applications. In the cloud storage, lots of storage nodes are connected by a network and provide a single virtualized space to applications. The controller node manages all of nodes participating in the cloud storage as well as monitors overall resource status, such as the storage usage, the network bandwidth, and the resource health. The client node helps applications to access their data over the cloud storage communicating with the controller node and storage nodes. Based on this traditional storage architecture, we add new modules to it to guarantee a balanced QoS level to all heterogeneous services.

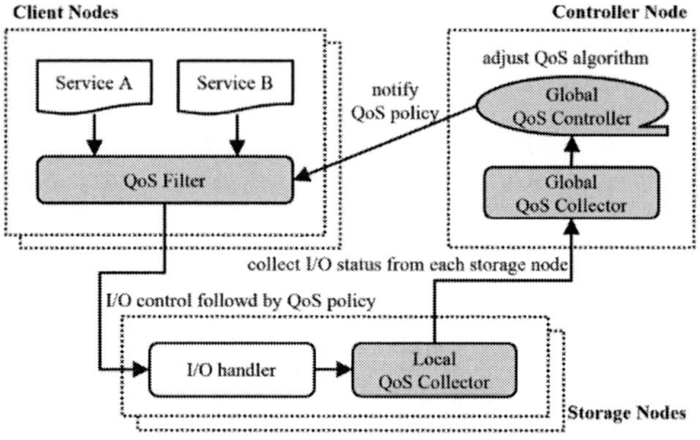

Figure 1. System Architecture

Local QoS Collector collects the local I/O history of all services in each node and forwards them to the controller node. The local I/O history can be collected by the I/O handler, which has a role of storing and retrieving an application data in the local storage media. Whenever the client node requests the data, the I/O handler notifies an access to information to the Local QoS Collector. There are two types of information in the local I/O history. One is the amount of access usage identified by each service and the other is each usage ratio of reading and writing within a service. All collected local I/O history is refreshed after notifying to the controller node in a specific period. One consideration point in notifying phase is how to decide the time interval to notify the local I/O history to the controller node. If the time interval is too short, it can give a burden to the system. On the contrary, if the time interval is too long, it becomes insensitive to workload changes so that a delayed QoS control is inevitable. However, because the time period does not undermine the basic functionality of our algorithm, we leave it to the tunable parameter.

Global QoS Collector manages a global I/O history collected from all storage nodes. That is, the global I/O history is the systemwide workload information which is merged with local I/O histories collected from storage nodes. After receiving the local I/O history from the local QoS collector, the global QoS collector classifies it by each service.

Global QoS Controller plays an important role to decide a policy for QoS control by using our algorithm. The global QoS controller analyzes system-wide workload information based on the global I/O history and decides a proper policy by using our Global QoS algorithm. For this, the Global QoS algorithm compares I/O workloads of each service to estimate the current I/O fairness level, such as the I/O skewness or the I/O starvation. After that, the Global QoS algorithm decides a policy for all services. If one of services is producing relatively bursty workload, a negative QoS policy is applied to that service. The negative QoS policy means that it tries to throttle overloaded workloads to an average access rate. Finally, determined policies are delivered to the client node to control the access behavior of the application.

QoS Filter is running on the client node and manages application access pattern based on policies decided by the global QoS controller. If one of the applications gets the negative policy, the QoS filter throttles the access speed of that application so as to keep all services to experience fair access quality.

B. Global QoS Algorithm

In this section, we explain the Global QoS algorithm to solve the I/O interference problem among multiple heterogeneous services in the cloud storage. The main principle of our algorithm is to control applications to use resources evenly within the uppermost system performance, which is dynamically renewed over time. We describe the algorithm in detail, as follows:

$$IO_{MAX} = MAX\left(IO_{MAX}(current), \sum_{s=1}^{s=n} HIST_{AVG}(T)\right) \quad (1)$$

We define the IO_{MAX} as the uppermost system performance in current hardware configuration. The service provider does not need to calculate the allowable performance value in their system, because our algorithm automatically updates the up-to-date IO_{MAX} by using real application workloads in (1). Under this equation, even if a new node is added to the cloud storage, our algorithm can update the IO_{MAX} for a new system configuration. For this, we use the $HIST_{AVG}$, which is the average access workload of each service for a period of T. The sum of all service's $HIST_{AVG}$ implies the total average usage of the cloud storage. Then, we compare the $HIST_{AVG}(T)$ with the current IO_{MAX}. If the current IO_{MAX} is less than the $HIST_{AVG}(T)$, we change the new IO_{MAX} with the calculated $HIST_{AVG}(T)$.

$$S_A = \left(\frac{IO_{MAX}}{Number\ of\ Services}\right) \quad (2)$$

The S_A(Allocation for a Service) means an allocated I/O quota for each service. The S_A can be calculated by dividing the IO_{MAX} to the number of services, as in (2). In our algorithm, every QoS policy is affected by the S_A value.

$$S_C = \left\{ \left(\frac{S_U - S_A}{S_A} \right) \times T \right\} \times \mathcal{M} \tag{3}$$

In (3), the S_U(Used value of a Service) means the amount used by the service in time T. The S_C(Control value for a Service) is used for controlling the service, which uses the storage resource excessively. Comparing the S_U with S_A, we decide a policy to perform the QoS control. If the S_U is less than the S_A, we provide a best-effort policy to allow full data access to that service. On the other hand, if the service usage exceeds the S_A, we consider that the QoS control is required to that service. In that case, we provide a negative policy to that service so that the global service fairness is guaranteed. For example, let us suppose that our algorithm allows services to use the cloud storage at a speed of 100MBps. If a service uses storage resources at a speed of 120MBps, we control the service to access data 20MBps slower. In addition, the $\mathcal{M}$ is used as a moderator to avoid fluctuation of the I/O performance caused by too sensitive access control. Using the $\mathcal{M}$, a smoother quality control is possible.

Procedure I : Calculating QoS Parameters from Real Workloads

```
Variables: current IO_MAX, HIST_AVG(T) for each service
Location: the Controller Node

Procedure WORKLOAD_CALCULATOR
  /* get sum of each service workloads */
  for each service 1 ~ N
    add HIST_AVG(T) ← "average I/O usage for each service"
  end loop

  /* get average workload value for all services */
  HIST_AVG(T) ← ( HIST_AVG(T) / N )

  /* get IO_MAX from real workloads */
  IO_MAX ← MAX(IO_MAX(current), HIST_AVG(T))

  /* get S_A which is an allocated quota for a service */
  S_A ← IO_MAX / N
End Procedure
```

Figure 2. Caculate QoS Prameters

Procedure II : Determine QoS Policy

```
Variables: S_A, S_U, T
Location: the Controller Node

Procedure POLICY_GENERATOR
  /* get S_C to determine the policy for this service */
  S_C ← (( S_U - S_A ) / S_A) x T

  /* adjust S_C by using Moderator Constant */
  S_C ← S_C x M

  /* get I/O Policy for this service */
  if S_U < S_A then
     SET "best-effort" policy
  else if S_U < S_A then
     SET "negative" policy
  end if
End Procedure
```

Figure 3. Determine the QoS Policy

Procedure III : Throttling Each Service's I/O Activities

```
Variables: I/O Policy, S_C
Location: the Client Node

Procedure WORKLOAD_CONTROLLER
  /* throttle each I/O by using the determined policy */
  if Policy = "best-effort" then
     return
  else if Policy = "negative" then
     delay I/O request by using S_C value
  end if
End Procedure

Procedure every read() and write()
  /* control I/O action for this service */
  call WORKLOAD_CONTROLLER

  /* do actual I/O process */
  call 'read()' or 'write()' to access the data
End Procedure
```

Figure 4. Control the Each Service's QoS

Because our algorithm is designed to be suitable to a general cloud storage architecture, it can be easily adapted to most current storage platforms without disturbing their own functionality. For this, we represent our algorithms by using pseudo codes in Figures 2 to 4.

C. Global Weighted-QoS Algorithm

The Global QoS algorithm considers that all services have equal right to access the storage resource. It can successfully distribute the overall storage bandwidth to all services evenly. However, in the real cloud world, there are various service requirements depending on different conditions, such as the service scale, the number of users or the data access pattern. While one may require a small amount of storage bandwidth, the other may want unlimited data access. To reflect this factor to the cloud storage, we provide another scheme called the Global Weighted-QoS algorithm.

$$SW_A = (IO_{MAX} \times W) \tag{4}$$

We define SW_A(Weighted Allocation for a Service) as an allocated I/O quota derived from applying the weight parameter to the IO_{MAX}. Although the weight parameter can be the storage usage ratio, the hard limited value of the I/O usage or any values influencing the storage performance, we regard the weight parameter as a storage usage ratio(%) to simplify the description. Under the weight parameter concept, each service can use the storage resource within the SW_A. The SW_A for a service can be calculated by (4).

$$SW_C = \left\{ \left(\frac{S_U - SW_A}{SW_A} \right) \times T \right\} \times \mathcal{M} \quad (5)$$

In (5), the SW_C is used for controlling the service, which excessively uses the storage resource compared to SW_A. The algorithm flow is very similar to the global QoS algorithm. If the SW_C is greater than the SW_A in time T, we control the access speed of that service.

IV. Performance Evaluations

In this section, we discuss the result of performance evaluations to verify our algorithms. Our simulation codes are added to the MAHA-FS [19], which was developed by ETRI in Korea. The MAHA-FS is a large scale distributed cloud storage for supporting high scalability, high reliability and a scaled up performance. MAHA-FS isolates each service by allocating independent volumes to store user data. Each volume provides the replication scheme to guarantee an available service. Currently, the MAHA-FS has been used in lots of real services, such as internet portals, content delivery network (CDN) services, and broadcasting companies. As a representative reference, we have UPlusBox [20], which is the biggest cloud service in Korea. UplusBox have been using 10PB of storage in single silo constructed by the MAHA-FS. As the accumulated storage capacity for all silos reaches about 60PB, MAHA-FS has been recognized as a reliable as well as a practical system.

A. Experimental Setup

Our evaluation environment is shown in Figure 5. This testbed is used for developing and testing of the MAHA-FS. There are 7 racks, each of which has 36-38 nodes respectively and a total of 256 nodes are connected within the cluster. Each node consists of the same hardware specifications: 2.5GHz X3320 CPU, 2GB of memory and 512GB hard disk. All machines run on Linux kernel 2.6.32 and are connected through a gigabit ethernet network. For a network configuration, the Extreme X650-24T runs as a core switch, and it is connected with 7 Extreme X350-24T edge switches.

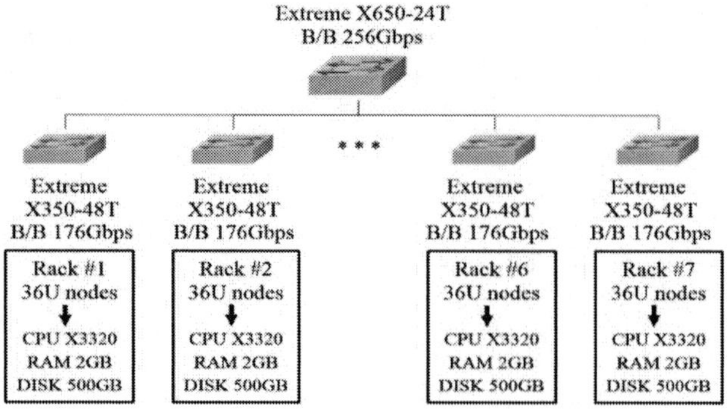

Figure 5. Evaluation Environment

B. Global QoS Control

To verify the Global QoS algorithm to guarantee the fairness for multiple heterogeneous services, we simulate our algorithm by using general Web service workloads. There are 4 services running simultaneously, and all services upload or download random files in the same manner. The size of each file is determined randomly in the range from 600MB to 1.4GB. To generate an imbalance of storage consumptions, we set each service to have different number of users. While the smallest service A has 100 users, the biggest service D has 400 users. Next, we observe before and after the performance transition under applying our algorithm.

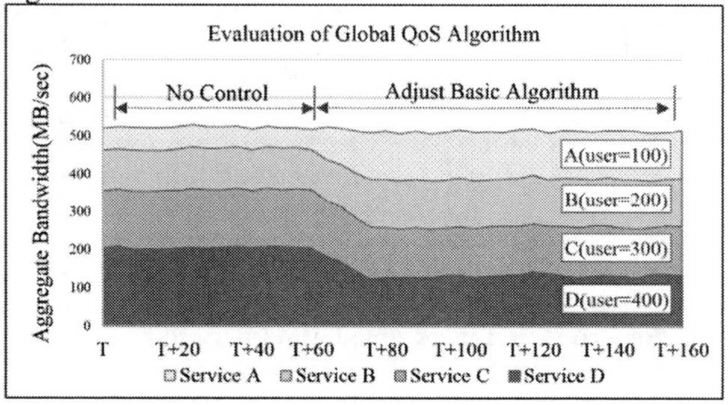

Figure 6. Fairness Result of the Global QoS Algorithm

In Figure 6, the X-axis is a time increased by second and the Y-axis means an occupied bandwidth for each services. Before T+60 without any control, we can see obviously unfair access results depending on the service scale. While service D uses the storage at the speed of 200MB/sec, service A only shows 30MB/sec. However, after applying our algorithm in T+60, each service is changed to have equal resource usage. Our algorithm analyzes a workload status, and lets all services to use a storage resource in fair way. The range from T+60 to T+80 is the intermediate period of adjustment. Our algorithm throttles the bandwidth of excessive services, such as service C and service D. And then, we can see that a sustained fair bandwidth is guaranteed for all services continuously.

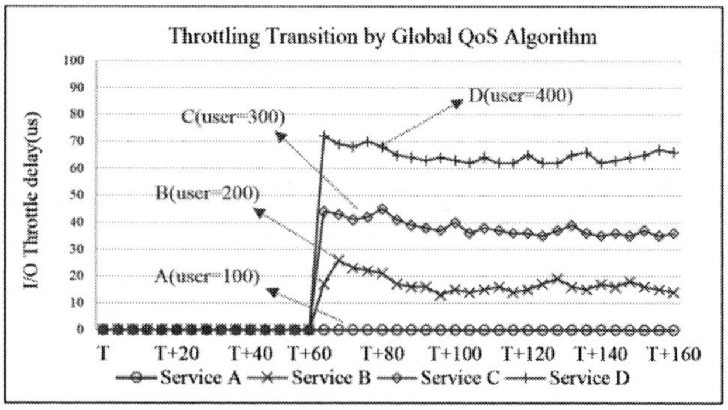

Figure 7. Throttling on the Global QoS Algorithm

Figure 7 shows the I/O throttle transition in the same simulation. Similar to Figure 3, we can see that access to excessive services is controlled after T+60. Especially, the I/O throttle value is increasing in proportion to the service scale. In case of the biggest service D, about 70us of throttle delay is assigned for every access. Another notable point is the degree of performance fluctuation caused by too sensitive throttling action. However, as can be seen in Figure 4, our algorithm guarantees a sustained QoS control over the whole period.

C. Global Weighted-QoS Control

In this section, we discuss the evaluation result of the Global Weighed-QoS algorithm. Unlike in Section B, we set all services to have the same workload. The whole simulation is performed in three stages; the first is the stage in which services are working without our algorithm, the second is the stage in which our algorithm is applied with a different weight value, and the third stage is the stage in which our algorithm is applied with the same weight value. To satisfy different workload demands, we set the weight value of { 5%, 15%, 30%, 50% } at the second stage and { 25%, 25%, 25%, 25% } at the third stage, respectively. Figure 8 shows the result of our Global Weighted-QoS algorithm. In first stage, all of services share the storage resource in fair way because all services run with the same workload. However, after applying our global weighted-QoS algorithm in T+60, we can see that the QoS control is successfully working.

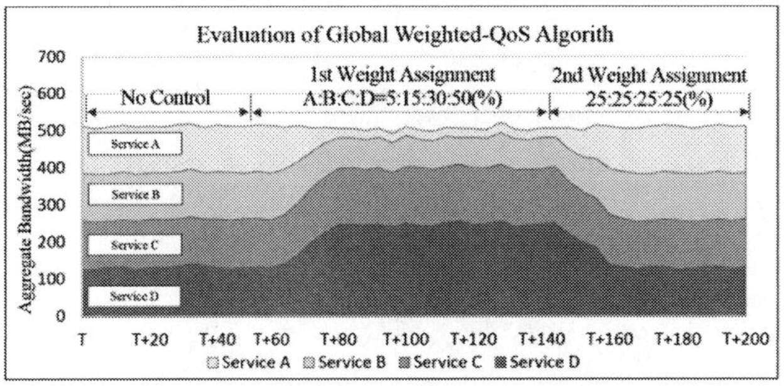

Figure 8. Throttling on the Global QoS Algorithm

Our algorithm analyzes the workload status of all services and automatically controls the QoS level of each service depending on the weight value. Finally, in T+140, all services share the resources in a fair way after applying the same weight value. Because the same weight value means that all services are controlled in a fair way, the result of the third stage is the same as the result of the first stage.

V. CONCLUSIONS

In this paper, we propose a workload adaptive I/O fairness scheme, which supports the global fairness among multiple heterogeneous services. The Global QoS algorithm guarantees balanced I/O performance regardless of service workloads. Our model has two contribution factors. The first is that the quality of service is guaranteed on storage level by using real workloads rather than higher layers, such as the application, the server, and the network. While traditional approaches require continuous optimizations for the cloud platform, our model controls the QoS in itself. The second contributing factor is that our idea has been designed to suit a general cloud storage architecture, and it can be easily adapted to many current storage platforms without disturbing their own functionality.

ACKNOWLEDGMENT

This work was supported by the ICT R&D program of MSIP/IITP, [R7117-16-0232, Development of extreme I/O storage technology for 32Gbps data services]

REFERENCES

[1] B. Calder, J. Wang, A. Ogus, N. Nilakantan, A. Skjolsvold, S. McKelvie, J. Haridas, "Windows Azure Storage: a highly available cloud storage service with strong consistency," Proceedings of the 23th ACM Symposium on Operating Systems Principles, pp. 143-157, Oct. 2011.

[2] Amazon Elastic Compute. [Online]. Available from: http://aws.amazon.com, Feb. 2017.

[3] K. Shvachko, H. Kuang, S. Radia, R. Chansler, R, "The hadoop distributed file system," IEEE 26th symposium on Mass storage systems and technologies (MSST), pp. 1-10, May. 2010.

[4] Openstack Networking. [Online]. Available from: http://wiki.openstack.org/Quantum. Feb. 2017.

[5] Apache Cloudstack. [Online]. Available from: http://www.cloudstack.org. Feb. 2017.

[6] Gartner 261942, Forecast Analysis: Public Cloud Services,

[7] SNIA, The Storage Networking Industry Association, [Online]. Available from: http://www.snia.org, Feb. 2017.

[8] Google App Engine, [Online]. Available from: https://appengine.google.com, Feb. 2017.

[9] A. Ghodsi, M. Zaharia, S. Shenker, I. Stoica, "Choosy: Max-min fair sharing for datacenter jobs with constraints," Proceedings of the 8th ACM European Conference on Computer Systems, pp. 365-378, April. 2013.

[10] M. Qureshi and Y. Patt, "Utility-based cache partitioning: A low-overhead, high-performance, runtime mechanism to partition shared caches," Proceedings of the 39th Annual IEEE/ACM International Symposium, pp. 423-432, Dec. 2006.

[11] Y. Xie and G. Loh, "PIPP: promotion/insertion pseudo-partitioning of multi-core shared caches," In ACM SIGARCH Computer Architecture News, pp. 174-183, June. 2009.

[12] R. Nathuji, A. Kansal, A. Ghaffarkhah, "Q-clouds: managing performance interference effects for qos-aware clouds," In Proceedings of the 5th ACM European conference on Computer systems, pp. 237-250, April. 2010.

[13] X. Pu, L. Liu, Y. Mei, S. Sivathanu, Y. Koh, C. Pu, "Understanding performance interference of i/o workload in virtualized cloud environments," IEEE 3rd International Conference on Cloud Computing, pp. 51-58, July. 2010.

[14] Y. Koh, R. Knauerhase, P. Brett, M. Bowman, Z. Wen, C. Pu, C, "An analysis of performance interference effects in virtual environments,", In Performance Analysis of Systems & Software. ISPASS 2007. IEEE International Symposium, pp. 200-209, April. 2007.

[15] A. Kumar, R. Rastogi, A. Silberschatz, B. Yener, "Algorithms for provisioning virtual private networks in the hose model," IEEE/ACM Transactions on Networking, pp. 565-578, 2002.

[16] M. Wachs, M. Abd-El-Malek, E. Thereska, G. Ganger, "Argon: Performance Insulation for Shared Storage Servers," in FAST, pp. 5-5, Feb. 2007.

[17] D. Shue, M. Freedman, A. Shaikh, "Performance Isolation and Fairness for Multi-Tenant Cloud Storage," In OSDI, pp. 349-362, Oct. 2012.

[18] H. Song, Y. Yin, X. Sun, R. Thakur, S. Lang, "Server-side I/O coordination for parallel file systems," In High Performance Computing, Networking, Storage and Analysis(SC). International Conference on IEEE, pp. 1-11, Nov. 2011.

[19] Y. Kim, D. Kim, H. Kim, Y. Kim, W. Choi, "MAHA-FS: A distributed file system for high performance metadata processing and random IO," KIPS Transactions on Software and Data Engineering, pp. 91-96, 2013.

[20] UPlusBox: the Biggest Cloud Service in Korea, [Online]. Available from: http://uplusbox.co.kr, Feb. 2017.

A Novel Location Estimation Method based on an Apollonian Circle with Robust Filtering

Byung-Jin Lee
Department of Electrical and Electronic Engineering, Chungbuk National University, Cheongju, Chungbuk, Rep. of Korea
Byung2487@naver.com

Byung-hoon Lee
Department of Electrical and Electronic Engineering, Chungbuk National University, Cheongju, Chungbuk, Rep. of Korea
qud7942@naver.com

Kyung Seok Kim
Department of Electrical and Electronic Engineering, Chungbuk National University, Cheongju, Chungbuk, Rep. of Korea
kseokkim@cbnu.ac.kr

***Abstract*— Noise, deviations, and outliers with varying distribution characteristics exist in measured data for outdoor location estimation, propagation characteristics that make source location estimation difficult. The estimation error of conventional methods (typically a least-squares method) is increased by such outliers. To solve this problem, this study proposes a novel location estimation method, specifically a modified trilateration technique based on Apollonian circles that does not require knowing the exact transmission power of the source or carrying out a calibration procedure. The proposed method results in improved location estimates compared to existing methods, which is confirmed with robust filtering in verification experiments.**

Keywords- Robust location estimation; received signal strength indication; random sample consensus; Apollonian circle

I. INTRODUCTION

Wireless geolocation refers to the problem of finding the location of mobile subscribers in different radio systems, such as cellular networks, wireless local area networks, and wireless sensor networks [1]. Researchers have proposed several methodologies for estimating the location of unknown radio frequency (RF) sources based on different physical characteristics, including received signal strength indication (RSSI), time-of-arrival (TOA), time-difference-of-arrival (TDOA), and angle-of-arrival (AOA). Of these, RSSI-based location estimation methods can be implemented easily with no additional hardware; thus, this method is frequently used. The main drawback to algorithms that use RSSI as a range measurement is that they are highly dependent on the propagation conditions that exist between the transmission point (TP) and each measurement point (MP).

The most widely used positioning mechanism is the Global Positioning System (GPS). GPS requires four or more satellite signals to function properly. These signals can be impossible to obtain indoors, in downtown city centers with tall buildings, under poor atmospheric conditions, or in geographically obstructed outdoor areas, such as deep valleys. Satellite-based localization services may also be disabled at any time by intentional jammers [2]. Therefore, new positioning techniques are needed in environments that cannot use GPS but require highly accurate, reliable results.

Moreover, a reliable location estimation algorithm must adapt to unknown channel conditions. For this reason, the least-squares (LS) method [3] is generally used to determine source location. However, this method generates significant error when using attenuated data based on the characteristics of the radio channel. Data exhibiting distinct distribution characteristics are referred to as outliers. Outlier data are a major factor that interferes with accurate location estimation. The random sample consensus (RANSAC) algorithm was proposed by Fischler and Bolles [4]; it performs local parameter estimation to search the inliers group after removal from a target estimated by identifying outliers. The method is effectively used for the estimation of various models [5][6]. Even when the ratio of outliers is very high compared to the inliers, this algorithm can be used for robust location estimation.

Exiting localization studies can be classified as either range-based or range-free. In range-based methods, the TP at an unknown location determines the distances to MPs based on signal strength; they then use trilateration [7]. These methods achieve high localization accuracy, but require the availability of line-of-sight (LOS) propagation conditions between any three MPs and the TP. Range-free methods rely only on the locations of MPs; they do not use the distances to these nodes. To determine the TP location, the centroid algorithm [8] uses information from neighboring *MPs* instead of distance information.

This paper presents a novel probability-based approach to estimating location based on Apollonian circles [9] that does not use any map information or calibration stage. The proposed algorithm modifies existing trilateration techniques for a field environment dealing with extensively physical phenomena. Outlier data are removed to improve performance by applying the RANSAC algorithm. We provide simulation results that compare the estimation performance of the original and improved algorithms.

The paper is organized into four sections. Section 2 provides the methodology for and Section 3 describes the results of a performance analysis. The main conclusions are listed in Section 4.

II. PROPOSED LOCATION ESTIMATION ALGORITHM

A. Training Phase

In this stage, the MP locations and RSS values are recorded from each environment to serve as the training data set. Assume that the number of MPs is N, there is one unknown TP, the locations of the MPs are denoted by $\{m_1, \dots, m_N\}$, and the location of the unknown TP is denoted by x. For simplicity, it is assumed that each MP is equipped with a non-directional antenna. We consider a log-distance path-loss model [10], which is widely used for the analysis of outdoor wireless channels. The measured RSS value at each MP, P_i, may be formulated as the following expression:

$$P_i = P_0 - 10\gamma \log_{10}\left(\frac{d_i}{d_0}\right) + n_i \tag{1}$$

where P_0 is the power measured at a reference distance d_0 from the TP, γ is a path loss index. n_i is a zero-mean Gaussian and unit variance. The values of γ can be set depending on the propagation environment. Consequently, this phase is generally accomplished with the direct inversion of (1), i.e.:

$$\hat{d}_i \overset{def}{=} d_0 10^{\frac{P_0 - P_i}{10\gamma}} \tag{2}$$

which is a maximum likelihood estimator of $\hat{d}_i$ [11], asymptotically unbiased (and normal) but biased for a finite sample.

B. Location Estimation Phase

Next, we apply the proposed algorithm with the calculated distance to estimate the location of the TP. In existing methods, the location of an unknown TP is estimated by means of the least squares criterion. The proposed location estimation method obtains the TP by a calculation based on an Apollonian circle. Figure 1 shows the Apollonian circle based on the ratio of the distance between MPs; Figure 2 shows the proposed location estimation method based upon these circles. The relationship between two MPs ((x_1, y_1), (x_2, y_2)), for which the distance ratio $a:b$ can be obtained based on the distance estimated using (2), and the estimated TP location (x, y) are represented in (5).

$$\sqrt{(x-m_{x,1})^2+(y-m_{y,1})^2} : \sqrt{(x-m_{x,2})^2+(y-m_{y,2})^2} = a:b \tag{5}$$

$$\sqrt{(x-m_{x,1})^2+(y-m_{y,1})^2} : \sqrt{(x-m_{x,3})^2+(y-m_{y,3})^2} = c:d \tag{6}$$

$$\sqrt{(x-m_{x,2})^2+(y-m_{y,2})^2} : \sqrt{(x-m_{x,3})^2+(y-m_{y,3})^2} = f:e \tag{7}$$

Rearranging the above equations, we have:

$$x^2+y^2-\frac{2(a^2m_{x,2}-b^2m_{x,1})}{a^2-b^2}x-\frac{2(a^2m_{y,2}-b^2m_{y,1})}{a^2-b^2}y+\frac{a^2m_{x,2}^2+a^2m_{y,2}^2-b^2m_{x,1}^2-b^2m_{y,1}^2}{a^2-b^2}=0 \tag{8}$$

where, $a:b$ is the ratio of distance MP_1 to MP_2. The internal division point $P(\cdot)$ and external division point $Q(\cdot)$ of the circle are as follows:

$$P_1\left(x=\frac{am_{x,2}+bm_{x,1}}{a+b}, y=\frac{am_{y,2}+bm_{y,1}}{a+b}\right) \tag{9}$$

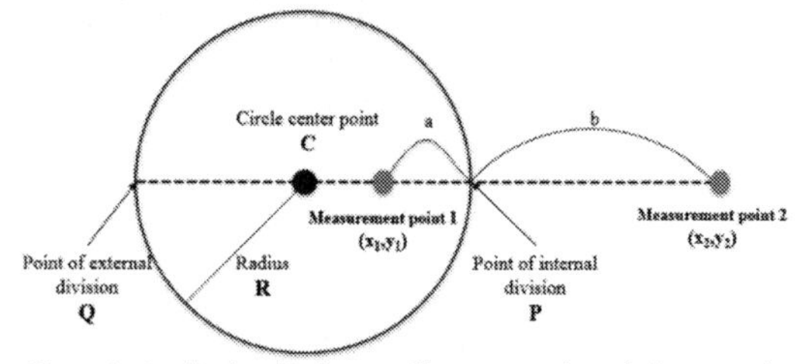

Figure 1. Apollonian Circle according to a certain ratio between the measurement points

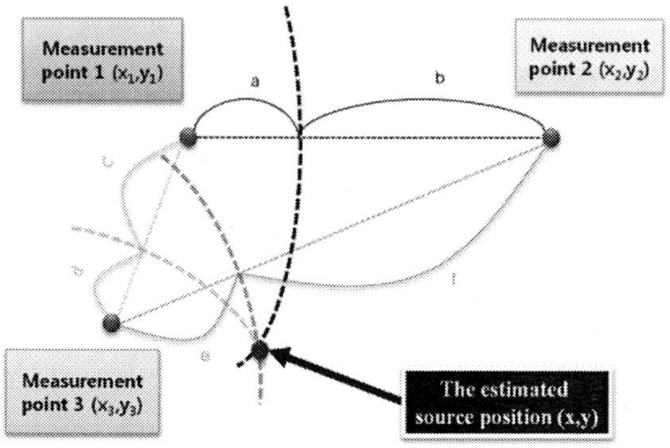

Figure 2. Proposed location estimation based on Apollonian circles

$$Q_1\left(x=\frac{am_{x,2}-bm_{x,1}}{a-b}, y=\frac{am_{y,2}-bm_{y,1}}{a-b}\right) \tag{10}$$

Through (9) and (10), the radius of the circle R and the center of the circle C can be determined as follows:

$$R_1=\frac{\sqrt{(P_{1,x}-Q_{1,x})^2+(P_{1,y}-Q_{1,y})^2}}{2}, \quad C_1\left(x=\frac{P_{1,x}+Q_{1,x}}{2}, y=\frac{P_{1,y}+Q_{1,y}}{2}\right) \tag{11}$$

Through (11), finally, the equation of a circle can be determined as follows:

$$\begin{aligned}(x-C_{1,x})^2+(y-C_{1,y})^2 &= R_1^2\\(x-C_{2,x})^2+(y-C_{2,y})^2 &= R_2^2\\(x-C_{3,x})^2+(y-C_{3,y})^2 &= R_3^2\end{aligned} \tag{12}$$

The circumference of a circle determined using (12) can be estimated to be the TP located between the two MPs. As seen in Figure 2, the TP (x, y) can be estimated by intersecting the circle between three or more MPs and a non-iterative solution can be found by linearizing the system. The results from (12) can be written in matrix form:

$$A\theta = \frac{1}{2}b \tag{13}$$

where

$$A=\begin{bmatrix} C_{1,x}-C_{2,x} & C_{1,y}-C_{2,y}\\ C_{1,x}-C_{3,x} & C_{1,y}-C_{3,y}\\ C_{2,x}-C_{3,x} & C_{2,y}-C_{3,y}\end{bmatrix}, \quad \theta=\begin{bmatrix}x\\y\end{bmatrix}$$

$$b = \begin{bmatrix} C^2_{1,x} - C^2_{2,x} + C^2_{1,y} - C^2_{2,y} - R_1^2 + R_2^2 \\ C^2_{1,x} - C^2_{3,x} + C^2_{1,y} - C^2_{3,y} - R_1^2 + R_3^2 \\ C^2_{2,x} - C^2_{3,x} + C^2_{2,y} - C^2_{3,y} - R_2^2 + R_3^2 \end{bmatrix} \quad (14)$$

where the set of A and b can be expressed in C_{xy} and R_{sh}, respectively, the solution equation is given by [12] :

$$\mathbf{z} = \left(C_{xy}{}^T C_{xy}\right)^{-1} C_{xy}{}^T R_{sh} \quad (15)$$

Next, the outliers in $\mathbf{z}$ are filtered by applying the RANSAC algorithm. First, k samples are selected from the random measurement data. The point in the parameter space is defined by repeatedly selecting random subsets of the data and generating model hypotheses for each subset. The number of data points below a pre-determined threshold value is calculated. After S repetitions of this process, the best score model B is returned as the solution. The RANSAC algorithm must determine two main parameters, the sampling number of iterations S and threshold T, of inliers and outliers. The number of repetitions needed to guarantee a success probability η_0 is calculated as follows [7]:

$$S \geq \frac{\log(1-\eta_0)}{\log(1-\rho^m)} \quad (16)$$

where the probability η_0 that at least one sample is selected from within the Sth inlier is typically set to 0.95 or 0.99; ρ is the percentage of inliers in the data; and m is the number of samples used to generate a hypothesis. The threshold value T can be selected empirically. If the residual variance of the inliers is σ^2, T is set to 2σ or 3σ. First, experimental data composed of inliers are applied to the RANSAC algorithm and the best approximation model is obtained. After obtaining the residual between the best approximation model and inliers, T is determined in proportion to this variance (or standard deviation). If the residual of the inliers is assumed to follow a normal distribution, when $T = 2\sigma$, 97.7% of inliers are included, and when $T = 3\sigma$, 99.9% of inliers are included. Finally, it is possible to obtain a refined solution equation from the inliers obtained by filtering the outliers in $\mathbf{z}$.

$$\hat{\mathbf{z}} = \left(\hat{C}_{xy}{}^T \hat{C}_{xy}\right)^{-1} \hat{C}_{xy}{}^T \hat{R}_{sh} \quad (17)$$

III. PERFORMANCE EVALUATION

In this section, estimation accuracy is tested in a field environment. The TPs were stationary and the RSSI dataset was acquired in practical experiments by car on the Korea Advanced Institute of Science and Technology (KAIST) campus in Daejeon, South Korea. The antenna was non-directional and fixed on the roof of the car, which moved at an average of 60 km/h. The resolution bandwidth was 12.5 KHz. Measurement data were stored every second. To reduce statistical variability, the saved data were averaged over 30 repetitions. The center frequencies of the RF signal used in our experiments was 421.5 MHz, the band used in amateur, industrial/business, public safety, and radio-location radio services. We used an arbitrary frequency from the amateur stations for the localization test. We set the TP, which transmitted a single tone signal, in the center of a building covering an area of 0.9 km × 0.95 km. Figure 3 shows the measurement environment, where the red dot is the actual TP and yellow line is the measurement path.

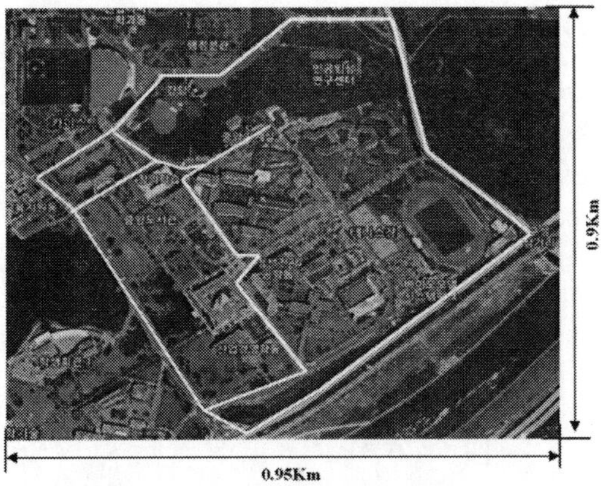

Figure 3. Measurement location in field environment

The simulation was performed 1000 times to represent the range of fluctuation in the distance error after the simulation. Figure 4a shows the probability density function (PDF) performance with or without the RANSAC algorithm. When the RANSAC is applied, the average estimated error distance is 21.16m, which is about 10.28m better than 31.44m without the RANSAC. Figure 4b is the cumulative distribution function (CDF) result of the proposed method with the RANSAC. The simulation resulted in a distance error range of 5–37.4 m, a mean distance error within 21.16 m, and a minimum distance error of 5.05 m. Figure 5 shows the location estimation methods used for performance comparison which are the trilateration [7] and triangle centroid location algorithms [8]. Tab. 1 summarizes the means and the 50th, 75th, and 90th percentile values of the error distance for each method. The proposed method performs better than both of the other methods, e.g., 50% of the distance error for the proposed method is within 20.62 m, compared with 129.36 m and 42.81 m for the trilateration and centroid methods, respectively. Similarly, for the proposed method, 90% of the distance error is within 28.18 m, and 157.25 m and 43.97 m for the trilateration and centroid methods.

If the measurement is performed in an outdoor environment, interference from a variety of factors is possible. Therefore, if position is estimated in an outdoor environment with only the RSSI value, the margin of error significantly increases. For the centroid method to result in precise localization, it must be widely distributed with a large number of MPs. However, its estimation performance is relatively poor in outdoor environments in which it is difficult to be widely distributed. Therefore, the centroid method is inefficient for use in high-precision localization. Trilateration is based on a simple

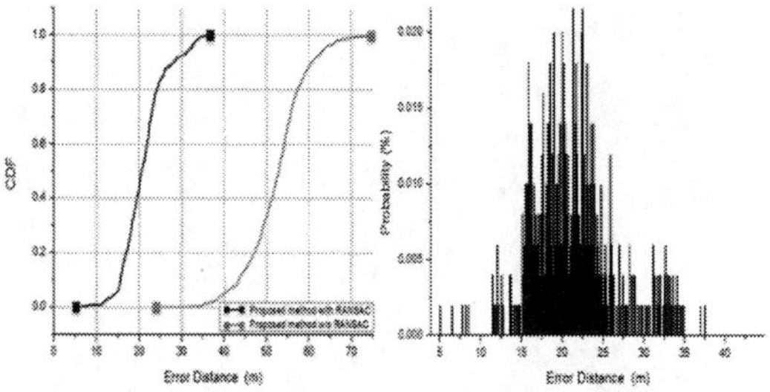

(a) (b)

Figure 4. PDF of the error distance of the proposed method, (a) Comparison of results with RANSAC, (b) PDF of the error distance of the proposed method

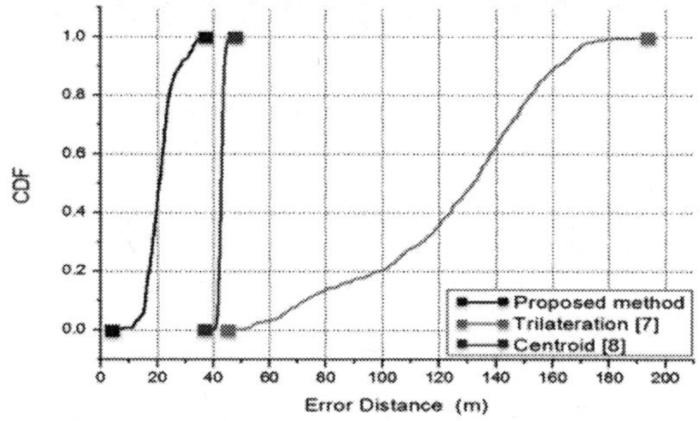

Figure 5. PDF of the error distance of the proposed method

TABLE I. ESTIMATION ERROR OF THE PROPOSED, TRILATERATION, AND CENTROID METHODS

	TRILATERATION [7]	CENTROID [8]	PROPOSED METHOD
MIN ERROR	42.75 m	39.7 m	5.05 m
MEAN ERROR	125.07 m	43.14 m	21.16 m
50th PERCENTRILE	129.36 m	42.81 m	20.62 m
75th PERCENTRILE	146.44 m	43.42 m	23.52 m
90th PERCENTRILE	157.25 m	43.97 m	28.18 m

mathematical calculation. Therefore, it is necessary to know the TP; if an error in distance estimation occurs due to obstacles between the TP and MP or in the surrounding environment, it is impossible to accurately estimate its position. In the proposed method, three or more TPs are calculated as a ratio of distances by applying the Apollonian circle. Therefore, it is possible to estimate position without the exact transmission power of the source, and precise position estimation compared with existing methods is made possible by removing outliers. In summary, in outdoor environments, it seems feasible to adopt our algorithm to estimate location based on the Apollonian circle scheme, which provides meaningful mapping of the topography in a large area.

IV. CONCLUSION

This paper presents a GPS-free scheme for outdoor localization. To overcome limitations caused by RSSI uncertainty, we describe a novel RSS-based outdoor location estimation method. The proposed scheme, based on Apollonian circles and RANSAC, improves upon both the accuracy and performance of conventional methods, particularly in complex environments. Additionally, it requires neither knowing the exact transmission power of the source nor any performing any calibration procedure. We verified our approach using computer simulation and practical experimentation, finding that the proposed algorithm has a considerable advantage in real-world precision and efficiency.

REFERENCES

[1] A. H. Sayed, A. Tarighat, and N. Khajehnouri, "Network-based wireless location: Challenges faced in developing techniques for accurate wireless location information," IEEE Signal Processing Magazine, vol. 22, no. 4, pp. 24–40, Jul. 2005.

[2] J. Peng, W. Falin, Z. Ming, W. Feixue, and Z. Kefei, "An improved GPS/RFID integration method based on sequential iterated reduced sigma point Kalman filter," IEICE Transactions on Communications, vol. E95-B, no.7, pp. 2433–2441, 2012.

[3] Y. Xu, J. Zhou, and P. Zhang, "RSS-based source localization when path-loss model parameters are unknown," IEEE Communications Letters, vol. 18, no. 6, pp. 1055–1058, 2014.

[4] M. A. Fischler and R. C. Bolles, "Random sample consensus: a paradigm for model fitting with applications to image analysis and automated cartography," Communications of the ACM, vol. 24, no. 6, pp. 381–395, 1981.

[5] L. Goshen and I. Shimshoni, "Guided sampling via weak motion models and outlier sample generation for epipolar geometry estimation," International Journal of Computer Vision, vol. 80, no. 2, pp. 275–288, 2008.

[6] C. M. Cheng and S. H. Lai, "A consensus sampling technique for fast and robust model fitting," Pattern Recognition, vol. 42, no. 7, pp. 1318–1329, 2009.

[7] G. Ferrari., Sensor Networks: Where Theory Meets Practice, Springer-Verlag, Berlin Heidelberg, 2010.

[8] L. Juan, W. Ke,L. Li, L. Chang-gang "Weighted centroid localization algorithm based on intersection of anchor circle for wireless sensor network", Journal of Ji Lin University, vol. 39, no. 6, pp. 1649–1653, 2009.

[9] J. Hoshen, "The GPS equations and the problem of Apollonius," IEEE Transactions on Aerospace and Electronic Systems, vol. 32, no. 3, pp. 1116–1124, Jul. 1996.

[10] Y. Liu, Z. Yang, X. Wang, and L. Jian, "Location, localization, localizability," Journal of Computer Science and Technology, vol. 25, no. 2, pp. 274–297, Mar. 2010.

[11] G. Wang, H. Chen, Y. Li, and M. Jin, "On received-signal-strength-based localization with unknown transmit Power and path loss exponent," IEEE Wireless Communications Letters, vol. 1, no. 5, pp.536-539, Oct. 2012.

[12] S. M. Kay, Fundamentals of Statistical Signal Processing: Estimation Theory, Prentice Hall, Inc., 1993.

Booters and Certificates: An Overview of TLS in the DDoS-as-a-Service Landscape

Benjamin Kuhnert*, Jessica Steinberger*†, Harald Baier*, Anna Sperotto† and Aiko Pras†

*da/sec - Biometrics and Internet Security Research Group
University of Applied Sciences Darmstadt, Darmstadt, Germany
Email:{Benjamin.Kuhnert, Jessica.Steinberger, Harald.Baier}@h-da.de

†Design and Analysis of Communication Systems (DACS)
University of Twente, Enschede, The Netherlands
Email:{J.Steinberger, A.Sperotto, A.Pras}@utwente.nl

***Abstract*—Distributed Denial of Service attacks are getting more sophisticated and frequent whereas the required technical knowledge to perform these attacks decreases. The reason is that Distributed Denial of Service attacks are offered as a service, namely Booters, for less than 10 US dollars. As Booters offer a Distributed Denial of Service service that is paid, Booters often make use of Transport Layer Security certificates to appear trusted and hide themselves inside of encrypted traffic in order to evade detection and bypass critical security controls. In addition, Booters use Transport Layer Security certificates to ensure secure credit card transactions, data transfer and logins for their customers. In this article, we review Booters websites and their use of Secure Socket Layer certificates. In particular, we analyze the certificate chain, the used cryptography and cipher suites, protocol use within Transport Layer Security for purpose of security parameters negotiation, the issuer, the validity of the certificate and the hosting companies. Our main finding is that Booters prefer elliptic curve cryptography and are using Advanced Encryption Standard with a 128 bit key in Galois/Counter Mode. Further, we found a typical certificate chain used by most of the Booters.**

***Keywords*—booters; certificates; distributed denial of service as a service; mitigation; tls.**

I. Introduction

Over the last years, Distributed Denial of Service (DDoS) attacks remain the top threat responsible for infrastructure and service outages [1]. The reason is that DDoS attacks are getting more sophisticated and more frequent whereas the required technical knowledge to perform these attacks decreases. One possibility to launch DDoS attacks is offered to non-technical users by websites referred to as Booters [2][3]. A user accesses a Booter website and chooses an attack plan that defines a number of attacks with a maximum attack duration each within a maximum period of time (expiration time) [4]. After the selection of an attack plan, the customer request is forwarded to a payment system (e.g., PayPal, BitCoin and credit card), which notifies the Booter when the amount of money is paid. This notification unblocks the customer and allows the customer to perform as many attacks as he/she wants in accordance to the attack plan. Besides the simplicity to buy and launch DDoS attacks against anyone on the Internet, Booters also use Transport Layer Security (TLS) to hide their attacks, evade detection, and bypass critical security controls [5][6]. In addition, Booters also secure their credit card transactions, data transfer and logins using TLS certificates in order to protect their customers.

The main intention of the TLS protocol and the Public Key Infractructure (PKI) is to give customers the confidence to complete their transactions using several trust indicators. However, the TLS protocol did not originally include the provision of a validated business identity within the TLS certificate and, as a result, the role of the Certification Authority (CA) is to pass trust. Moreover, CAs should have a responsibility to ensure they only ever issue TLS certificates to legitimate companies. As opposed to this, Booters that use a TLS certificate to secure their Internet transactions are intended to generate harmful traffic against a target system.

In this paper, we review the use of TLS certificates of current Booters. Further, we analyze the characteristics of the used of TLS certificates (e.g., certificate chain, used cryptography and cipher suites, negotiation protocol, issuer and the validity of the certificate). To summarize, our contributions are as follows: i) We identify and classify the used TLS certificates of Booters and generalize potential malicious certificate chains; ii) We study in detail the characteristics of the used TLS certificates (e.g., used cryptography and cipher suites, negotiation protocol, issuer and the validity of the certificate) and uncover same Booter infrastructures; iii) We discuss strategies to mitigate Booters using TLS certificates.

II. Booters and SSL certificates

In this section, we provide a general overview of Booters using TLS certificates. First, we define the terminology that is used throughout this paper and describe the methodology to retrieve the TLS certificate. Second, we provide information regarding the certificate chain, the used cryptography and cipher suites, protocol use within TLS for purpose of security parameters negotiation, the issuer and the validity of the certificate. We aim to shed light onto the typical TLS configuration parameters of Booter websites and discuss our findings in terms of mitigation and response to DDoS attacks.

A. Terminology

The analysis of Booter websites has revealed that there are various terms used to describe websites that offer DDoS-as-a-Service. Namely, Booters websites are also known as

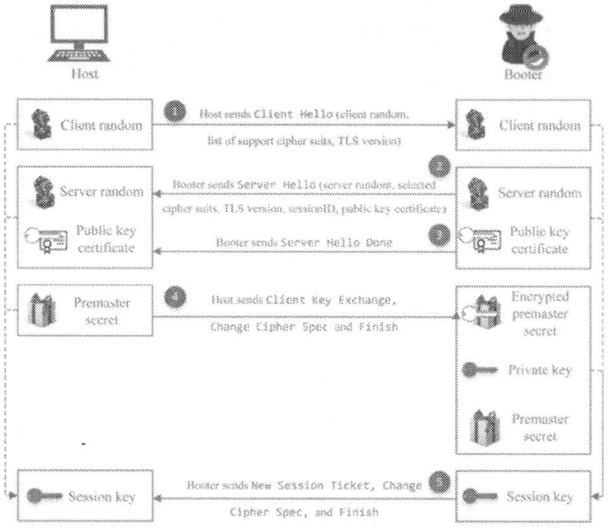

Figure 1. SSL handshake with a Booter website.

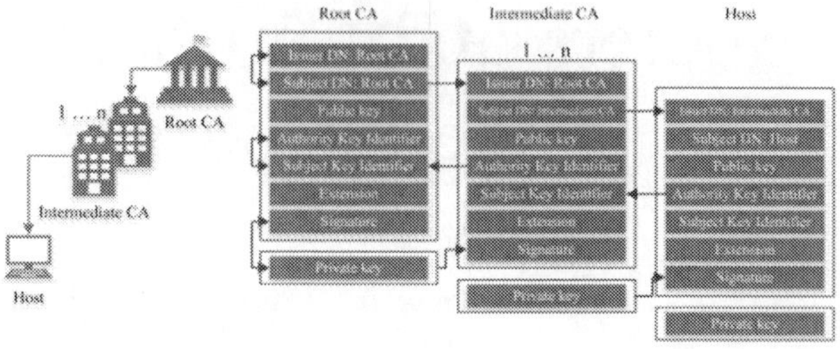

Figure 2. Certificate chain and linkages between certificates [13].

Stressers, DDoS-for-hire, DDoS-as-a-Service, and DDoSers [4]. In this paper, we adhere to the term Booter and refer to the infrastructure of a Booter presented in [4].

Further, we adhere to the definition of a CA by [7]: "A certification authority is a general designation for any entity that controls the authentication services and the management of certificates. A CA can be public commercial, private or personal. CAs are independent and define an Certification Practice Statement (CPS)."

B. Methodology

First, we monitor the landscape of Booter websites that listen to HyperText Transport Protocol Secure (HTTPS) requests and reply with a TLS certificate to secure their Internet transactions based on the Booterblacklist [8]. To connect to a Booter website, we first used the TLS client program `s_client` of OpenSSL. However, we found that the OpenSSL program `s_client` is not always able to extract and store the certificate chain of an existing connection. To overcome missing certificate chains, we developed two different TLS client programs and performed a TLS handshake [9] as shown in Figure 1. The reason to develop two different TLS client programs is that the Booters website presents different TLS certificates during the SSL handshake based on the use of the Server Name Indication (SNI) Extension of SSL [10]. Therefore, one TLS client program makes use of the SNI Extension and the other program works without. We stored the cipher suits, TLS version, the Booters public key certificate and its certificate chain, and the Subject Alternative Name (SAN) field [11]. In addition to the TLS data, we used `whois` to query all domain name entries within the SAN field of the certificates to gather information about the hoster of the Booter websites.

C. The use of TLS certificates by Booter websites

Out of 434 Booters, 152 replied with a TLS certificate. Even though this amount is significantly less than the usage of TLS certificate authorities for the top 10 million websites presented in [12] (e.g., W3Techs [12] reported that 67.4% of the websites currently use TLS certificates), Gartner believes that by 2017 more than 50% of the network attacks will use SSL encryption [5]. As a result, the number of Booters that use TLS might also increase [6] .

1) Depth of TLS certificate chain: As described in [11], TLS certificates are built in a top down process. First, the self-signed Root CA certificate is established [13]. Next, the Root CA signs an intermediate CA certificate. This intermediate CA either create an additional intermediate CA or issues a certificate to people or hosts. To establish a valid certificate chain at least one CA is required. [13] reported that there is no theoretical maximum of certificate chains, but the average certificate chains have between two and three CAs in the hierarchy. The depth count is "level 0:peer certificate", "level 1: CA certificate", "level 2: higher level CA certificate", and so on. The last certificate is called Root certificate. In contrast to the process of building TLS certificates, the validation of TLS certificates is a bottom up approach. Both the building and verification process are shown in Figure 2. On average, Booter websites have a depth count of 4.

2) Geographic Distribution of TLS certificates: We examined the geographic distribution of the host, intermediate and root TLS certificates by using the subject and issuer two-letter International Organization for Standardization (ISO) country code and compared our findings with [2]. Our findings revealed a similar distribution of the top 10 two-letter ISO country code of the certificate's subject and issuer as reported by [2]. The top ranked country that issues TLS certificates to Booter websites is Sweden, followed by Great Britain. The geographical distribution of the TLS certificate by subject and issuer country is listed in Table I and shown in Figure 3. Surprisingly, the majority (74.59%) of the Booter websites that use TLS certificates provide the country code of the certificate subject and issuer. In addition to Table I, 10 certificates did not provide information about the subject and issuer country. Even though the country code is missing, the TLS certificate is still valid as the country name attribute is optional [11].

3) Types of TLS certificates: Besides self-signed certificates, currently three types of commercial TLS certificates

TABLE I. GEOGRAPHICAL DISTRIBUTION OF THE TLS CERTIFICATE BY USING THE SUBJECT AND ISSUER COUNTRY.

Country Name	BE	FR	GB	SE	US	ZA
Frequency	27	3	222	230	69	24

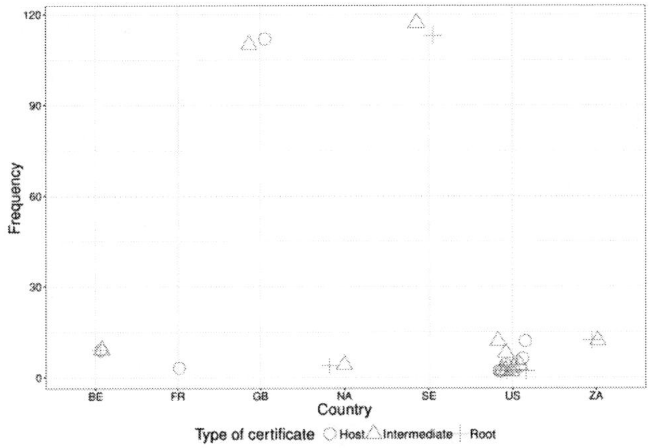

Figure 3. Geographic distribution of Booter's certificate issuer.

are available: Domain Validated (DV), Organization Validated (OV) and Extended Validation (EV).

The DV SSL certificate is the most common type of TLS certificate. The CA verifies only the domain name and typically exchanges confirmation email with an address listed in the domain's WHOIS record. DV certificates are typically verified and issued through automated processes. Human intervention is minimized and organization checks are eliminated in order to support issuing certificates in a quick and cheap manner. While the browser displays a padlock, examination of the certificate will not show the company name as this was not validated. All Booters listed on the Booter blacklist that respond to an HTTPs request make use of DV TLS certificates.

In contrast to DV certificates, CAs must validate the company name, domain name and other information through the use of public databases when issuing an OV certificate. The issued certificate will contain the company name and the domain name, for which the certificate was issued for. None of our Booter websites that use TLS certificates to secure their Internet transactions make use of a OV certificate.

The purpose of an EV certificate is to identify the legal entity that controls a website and to assist in addressing problems related to phishing, malware, and other forms of online identity fraud. An EV certificate is only issued once an entity passes a strict authentication procedure. The Guidelines for the Issuance and Management of Extended Validation Certificates [14] present criteria established by the CA/Browser Forum for use by certification authorities when issuing, maintaining, and revoking certain digital certificates for use in Internet website commerce. As in the OV, the EV lists the company name in the certificate itself. However, a fully validated EV certificate will also show the name of the company or organization in the address bar itself, and the address bar is displayed

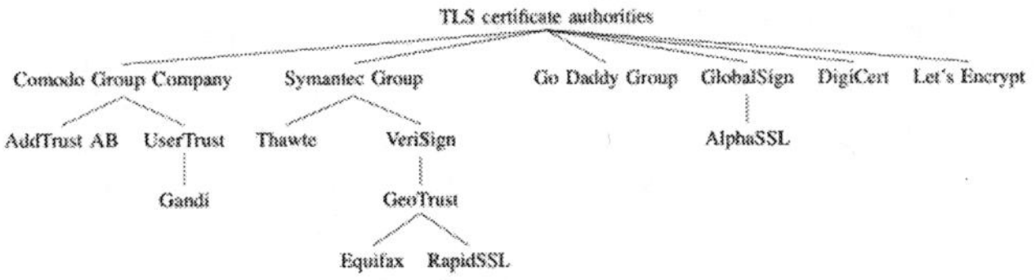

Figure 4. Relationship of TLS certificates.

in green. Further, other disambiguating information is also provided (e.g., address of Place of Business, Jurisdiction of Incorporation or Registration and Registration Number).

4) Certificate chain: In this section, we analyze the certificate chain of the TLS certificates used by the Booter websites. We found 585 TLS certificates used by 152 Booter websites as host, intermediate or root certificate issued by 17 different organizations. We recognized the occurrence of similar certificate chains and built an overview of relationships between CAs and their TLS certificates.

In a first step, we analyzed the root certificates and trusted CAs. At least for the European context, an EU Trusted Lists of Certification Service Providers is available. We compared the root certificates used by the Booter websites with the CAs listed on the EU Trusted List [15]. We assumed to find the majority of the root certificates used by Booter websites on the EU Trusted List as the geolocation revealed Great Britain and Sweden the top issuer countries as shown in Figure 3. However, the organization names of the root certificates of the Booter websites are not listed on the EU Trusted List of Certification Service Providers.

To answer the question of who is issuing the TLS certificates used by Booter websites, we built an overview of relationships between CAs and their TLS certificates as shown in Figure 4. The majority of the Booters intermediate and root certificates are issued by Comodo CA Limited and AddTrust AB.

However, AddTrust AB no longer exists as a company [16]. After ScandTrust, a private Swedish CA, acquired AddTrust AB, Comodo CA Limited purchased the AddTrust root certificates from ScandTrust [16]. Further, Comodo CA Limited also purchased the CA UserTrust [17], which had four roots [16]. As reported by [16], the key material was removed from its original sites of operation and transferred into Comodo's data and backup centers.

The next higher amount of TLS certificates are issued by organizations belonging to the Symantec Group. In 2000, Thawte was acquired by Symantec [18]. In the year 2006, VeriSign acquired GeoTrust [19] and bought the certificates from them. In 2010, Symantec acquired VeriSign's identity and authentication business for 1.28 billion US dollar [20] and thus owns the TLS and code signing certificate services, the managed public key infrastructure services, the VeriSign trust seal, the VeriSign identity protection authentication service and the VIP fraud detection service.

As a response to occurring security incidents in the past, some CAs are sold. Even though CAs are sold and their key material is transferred to other CAs, each of the hundreds of different root CAs are equally trusted by the browsers [21].

5) Costs of SSL certificates: The costs of a TLS certificate depend on the type of the certificate, the value of the used intermediate and root CAs within the certificate chain and the reputation of the issuing CA.

As described in Section II-C3, the three types of commercial TLS certificates DV, OV and EV are available. The cheapest certificate is a DV certificate (e.g., starting from $8.95 for a single domain and $98 for multiple domains), followed by the OV certificate (e.g., starting from $38 for a single domain and $180 for multiple domains). The most expensive TLS certificate is EV (e.g., starting from $99 for a single domain and $269 for multiple domains), because an applying entity has to pass strict authentication procedures.

In recent years, incidents with CAs that issued bogus TLS certificate have been published and discussed. In 2008, Eddy Nigg ordered an SSL certificate for Mozilla.com on CertStar's site without having to go through any validation or verify that he was authorized to order the certificate [22][23]. In the year 2011, a Comodo affiliate RA was compromised resulting in the fraudulent issue of 9 SSL certificates to sites in 7 domains [24][25]. Later in 2011, the DigiNotar CA detected an intrusion into its CA infrastructure, which resulted in the fraudulent issuance of 531 public key certificate requests for a number of domains, including Google.com [26][27]. In 2015, Microsoft revoked an improperly issued SSL certificate for the domain `live.fi` that could be used in attempts to spoof content, perform phishing attacks, or perform man-in-the-middle attacks [28][29].

In most of the aforementioned cases, the involved CA that issued bogus TLS certificates have been sold or dissolved and their key material has been transferred to different parties. The acquiring organization recognized the lower value of such a CA, offer these TLS certificates to third party vendors that sell these at a cheaper cost as the in-house generated ones [16]. As the Booter websites main intention is to earn money, most of the Booter websites make use of low-cost TLS certificates, as they are equally trusted by the browsers.

6) Serial numbers, wildcards and SAN of TLS certificates: Each TLS certificate must have a serial number, which uniquely distinguishes it from all other certificates issued by the same CA. The serial number is unique only to the issuing CA and a non-negative integer [11]. We analyzed 152 Booter Unified Resource Locators (URLs) and their certificate serial number. Out of 152 Booters URLs, 18 TLS certificates provide the same serial number to different Booter URLs as listed in Table II.

To ensure that these Booter URL are related to each other, we reviewed the common name and the alternative domain name attributes as the TLS certificate could be a wildcard or a Subject Alternative Name (SAN) certificate. Wildcard TLS certificates protect unlimited subdomains with a single certificate. In contrast to wildcard TLS certificates, SAN certificates protect multiple domain names with a single certificate. For example, a SAN certificate could be issued for `abc.de`. In addition, the domain `gef.hi` is added to the SAN values

TABLE II. DUPLICATE SERIAL NUMBERS OF USED TLS CERTIFICATES.

#	Serial number	URL
1	1121936FEA6ABA378CA723245B8F125A7850	booter-sales.hourb.com stresser.org
2	1121B4A4D767765C56B0224767AB1AE0767C	omega-stresser.us onestress.com
3	2FFF	darkstresser.weebly.com opaquebooter.weebly.com
4	55F2EBB7F44E0B5AC0125A5D14E72035	buyddos.com freezystresser.nl getsmack.de optimusstresser.com superstresser.com xrstresser.net
5	9D8646B2096A20FF0C48F24CEC1810EB	equinoxstresser.net riotstresser.com
6	BBBA942BA2268EF9A74B78A5D4412E8E	powerstresser.com signalstresser.com
7	109DFF6A138BB2677C35C5F6DAB7B089	crazyamp.me iddos.net

and thus the same certificate protects multiple domains. We identified the use of one wildcard certificate by the Booter infrastructure listed in Table II row 2. Further, we assume that the remainder of Booters in Table II use SAN certificates, but do not explicitly add the different Booter URLs to the alternative domain name attributes to secure their own Booter infrastructure. As reported by [2], Booters protect themselves using DDoS Protection Services. In case, the operator of a Booter infrastructure would enter all possible alternative domain names in the SAN attributes of a TLS certificate, the Booter infrastructure itself would be more vulnerable to attacks.

7) Certificate validity and revocation: When a TLS certificate is issued, it is expected to be in use for its entire validation period. However, various circumstances may cause a certificate to become invalid prior to the expiration of the validity period (e.g., change of name, change of association between subject and CA, a compromise or suspected compromise of the corresponding private key). In any of the aforementioned circumstances, the CA needs to revoke the certificate [11].

Common name: The Common Name (CN) of a TLS certificate is typically composed of a String containing the host and domain name [30]. The CN must be the same as the Web address that will be accessed when connecting to a secure site. As a consequence, the TLS certificate is valid only if the request host name matches either the common name or at least one of the certificate subject alternative names. We found that the 8 Booter URLs do not match to the CN written in the TLS certificate. As a result, the connections to this Booter websites appear to be invalid within the Browser. In a second step, we analyzed what kind of third party is used as CN of the certificate and found that the entries 1 and 4 in Table II use a CN or SAN of a domain parking company instead of the Booters URL.

Domain parking is often an advertising practice that resolve to a Web page containing advertising listings and links and are not limited to benign applications. However, the revenue

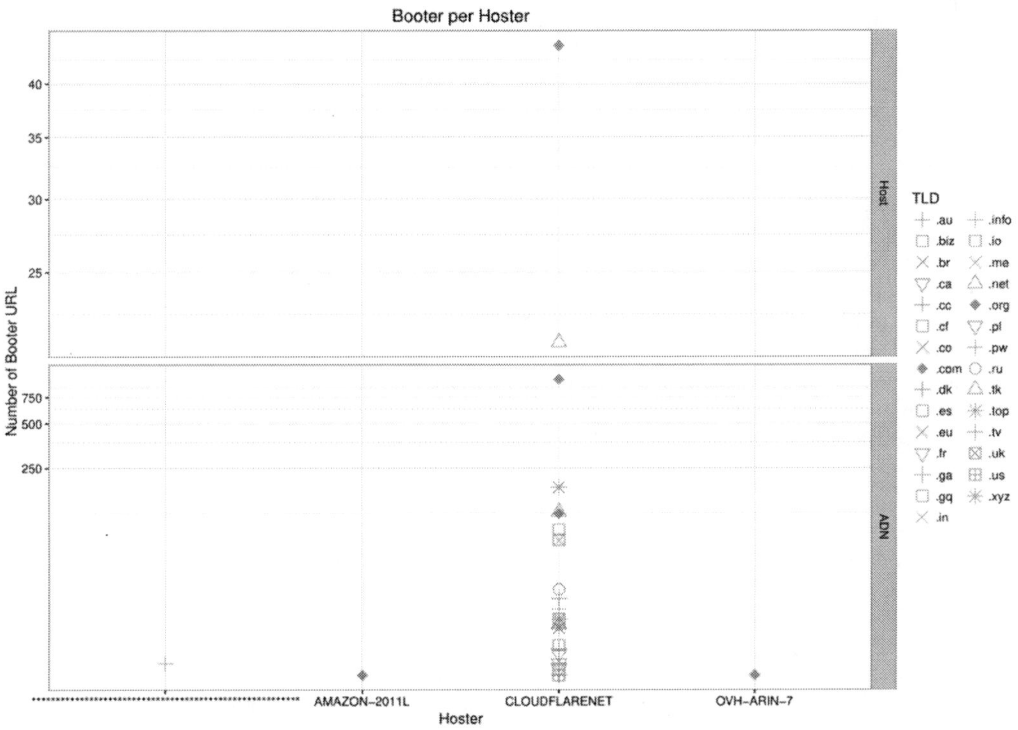

Figure 5. Distribution of Booter websites per Hoster.

generated is split between the parking service and the domain owner. As reported in [31] such domain parking monetization is a million-dollar business. In accordance with [32], we assume that domain parking is used by the owner of the Booter websites once malicious actions of these domains have been discovered and the domain has been blocked. Even though the malicious domains have been blocked, traffic from backlinks is still used to make money [32].

SAN: The Subject Alternative Name (SAN) field [11] within the TLS certificate specifies additional subject identifies. In case a SAN is defined, the SAN must always be used and the CN is only evaluated in case the SAN is not present. We found that Booter websites entered 21 additional subject identifies on average. Surprisingly, we also found Booter websites using more than 90 SANs in a single certificate. One possible explanation for this huge amount of SANs within a certificate is that these URLs reside in a Content Delivery Network (CDN) network. However, CDNs serve content on behalf of other companies. The servers of a CDN usually handle results of hundreds or thousands of different domains and are distributed all over the world. For reason of usability, these servers often share a single TLS certificate. Another explanation is that domains also might get compromised by Booter owners and are abused for malicious activities.

Validity period: Each TLS certificate contains a validity period. A validity period is described as the time interval during, which the CA warrants that it will maintain information about the status of the certificate [11]. A maximum validity period is described within the Baseline Requirements for the Issuance and Management of Publicly-Trusted Certificates by the CA/ Browser Forum [33] and is set to 39 months maximum validity of OV and DV TLS certificates in order to increase TLS security. However, the TLS certificates used by Booter websites use a maximum validity of half a year to one year on average.

Revocation: In Section II-C5, we presented some incidents with CAs that issued bogus TLS certificate. In most of those cases, the CA creates and disseminates revocations of the bogus TLS certificates. To revoke certificates nearly every certificate contains a reference to a Certificate Revocation List (CRL). A CRL is a list of certificates that the CA has revoked for whatever reason. However, [34] reported that browsers often do not bother to check whether certificates are revoked (including mobile browsers, which uniformly never check). Out of 152 Booter websites, only one Booter used a certificate that had been revoked. Browsing this Booter website raises an error message within the Web browser.

8) TLS protocol and cipher suites: During the TLS handshake the used cipher suite is negotiated. Our TLS client program uses a version-flexible SSL/TLS method and thus the protocol version used will be negotiated to the highest version mutually supported by the client and server. In total, our TLS client offered 42 cipher suites [35], from which a Booter website selects the one most appropriate. Out of 152 Booter websites that use TLS, 148 make use of TLS using a cipher suite in Galois Counter Mode (GCM) [36][37]. In particular, 146 Booter websites secure their websites using the elliptic curve cipher suite `ECDHE-ECDSA-AES128-GCM-SHA256`. According to the NIST recommendations on key length [38], a 256-bit elliptic curve key provides as much protection as a 3 072-bit asymmetric key.

9) Hoster of Booter websites: In order to identify the hosting provider of the Booter websites, we used the Booter URLs presented in the Booter blacklist and performed a `whois` query. We found that the majority of Booter websites that are using TLS reside in the CDN of Cloudflare. Figure 5 shows the distribution of Booter URLs within the hosting provider network categorized by Host or Alternative Domain Names (ADNs). For example, the majority of Booter websites make use of the Top Level Domains (TLDs) `.com` and `.net` and reside in the network of Cloudflare. Further, Figure 5 shows, in which network the SANs are hosted. We found that the majority of SANs presented within the TLS certificate of a Booter website also reside in the network of Cloudflare.

To validate our results, we compared the preferred used TLS protocol and cipher suite of the hosting network. In Section II-C8, we showed that the majority of Booter websites are using Elliptic Curve Cryptography (ECC) and GCM. This finding is in accordance with [39], who reported Cloudflare enables their customers to use ECDSA certificates on their CloudFlare-enabled sites. As a result, the majority of Booter websites using ECC and GCM reside in the network of the content delivery network Cloudflare.

10) TLD of Booters: Each Booter website is accessible via an URL that is registered though a registrar at ICANN. According to [40], 1930 Generic Top-Level Domains (gTLDs) are coordinated by ICANN. We reviewed the top level domains that are used by Booters websites. Reviewing the TLDs of the Booter URLs at depth 0, the majority of Booters use `.com` and `.net` TLDs. Taking also into account the SANs within the TLS certificate of a Booter website, the majority of TLDs are registered within the `.com`, `.xyz`, `.org`, `.net` and `.cf`. However, the number of registered domains within a TLD also vary and thus we reviewed the share of Booter URLs that use TLS compared to the overall amount of registered domains. Under consideration of the overall amount of registered domains, the majority of Booter URLs that use TLS registered a `.cf` domain followed by `.xyz`, whereas `.cf` is a country-code domain sponsored by the *Société Centrafricaine de Télécommunications (SOCATEL)* and the `.xyz` is a generic domain sponsored by XYZ.COM LLC.

III. Discussion

In this section, we provide an aggregated overview of the key findings. Further, we discuss our results with regard to possible mitigation strategies. We have summarized the information presented in Section II-C in Table III.

TABLE III. Summary of the use of TLS in the DDoS-as-a-Service landscape.

Criterion	Result
Use of TLS	152 of 434 (35%)
Depth of certificate chain	4
Geographic distribution of subject and issuer	Sweden, Great Britain
Type of TLS certificate	DV
Top certificate issuer	Comodo Group
# SANs	⌀21
Validity of certificate	0.5 – 1 year
Revoked	1 of 585 certificates
Preferred TLS protocol	TLSv1/SSLv3
Preferred TLS cipher suite	`ECDHE-ECDSA-AES128-GCM-SHA256`
Preferred TLDs	`.cf, .xyz`
Hoster (Host/ADN)	Cloudflare/Cloudflare

Even though the main intention of the TLS protocol and the PKI is to give customers the confidence to complete their transactions using several trust indicators, there are no technical restrictions in place that prohibit a CA from issuing a certificate to a malicious third party [21]. Thus, both the integrity of the CA based public key infrastructure and the security users' communications depend upon hundreds of CAs around the world choosing to do the right thing. As a consequence, anyone of those CAs can become the weakest link in the chain.

In case of occurring security incidents at a CA, the affected certificates should be revoked instead of selling the issuing CAs and their key materials to third parties. As a consequence, these TLS certificates are less valuable and are sold by the acquiring companies for a lower price. However, acquiring a CA and the transfer of key materials should be transparent to the users of the PKI and well documented for later lookups.

Further, the TLS certificates and PKI should provide non-technical users the possibility to differentiate low-value TLS certificates from high-value TLS certificates in order to decide, which URL to trust. At least for the European context, a list of trusted CAs is available. In order to decide whom to trust, a global list of trusted CAs would be beneficial. Besides the differentiation of low and high-value TLS certificates, the addition of a reputation level of CAs within the trusted list should be established.

Next, we found that the majority of TLS certificates used by Booter URLs are issued by the Comodo Group Company. According to [41], Comodo indeed is leading the overall market (33.6%), however Symantec is still stronger among top ranked websites. One possible mitigation strategies might be the removal of certain certification chains, but removing intermediate and root certificates from the trust store of the browser might cause a negative impact for non-technical users. As a consequence, there is clearly a need to provide the possibility to differentiate between different levels of trust for non-technical users and to improve usability of TLS certificates.

We found that in some cases Booter URLs do not match their SANs or CN within the TLS certificate. Current Web browsers raise a warning, but non-technical users might accept the exception shown in the Web browser and can access the website as expected. One approach to block the use of Booter websites and thus mitigate the effects caused by Booter attacks is to implement an automatic check and comparison of the CN and SANs with the Booters URL.

Besides the not matching SANs or CN with the Booter URL, we found that the Booter websites that use a TLS certificate specified 21 SANs on average. In total, we found 3 156 SANs specified within the TLS certificate of the Booter URLs listed on the Booter blacklist. Within these SANs, we identified further suspicious domain names that contain various terms to describe a Booter (e.g., www.beststresser.com uses also the SAN of *.bestipstressers.com). We suggest to use the SANs provided in each TLS certificate to extend the Booter blacklist. We also identified several TLS certificates that provide more than 90 SANs. One explanation might be that this Booter URL resides in a CDN network. For reasons of usability, CDN often share a single TLS certificate.

We identified numerous Booter URLs that reside in CDN networks. Even though these Booter websites carry out DDoS attacks and thus cause network traffic within the CDN network, in accordance with [42][43], we assume the amount of network traffic caused by these attacks is such that the CDN network operators might not be able to detect these DDoS attacks as their effects might be to small.

IV. Related work

Over recent years, DDoS-as-a-Service gained an increasing research interest. [2] analyzed attacks generated by 14 distinct Booter websites. Therefore, Santanna et al. [2] analyzed the attack types, the attack volume and the geographic distribution of the Booters. They found that DDoS-as-a-Service offers non-technical skilled users the possibility to perform DDoS attacks. In total, the authors were able to achieve up to 1.6 Gbps Domain Name System (DNS)-based and up to 7.0 Gbps CharGen attack traffic. In [3], the authors provide an overview of 15 operational MySQL databases (including users, attacks and infrastructures) of Booters. Besides the operational databases, Steinberger et al. [4] presented the Booter's scenario elements and their relationships. A Booters' scenario consists of the six elements: A Booter customer, a payment system, a database, a Booter website including DDoS Protection Service, a Booter infrastructure and a target system.

To mitigate DDoS attacks performed by Booter websites, a list of Booter characteristics to detect and classify them was created in the work of [44]. An initiative to share the (most extensive) list of websites that offer DDoS attacks as a paid service is provided on http://booterblacklist.com. However, none of the aforementioned works focused on the use of TLS certificates used by Booter URLs as one possible mitigation strategy.

V. Conclusions

In this paper, we conducted a structured analysis of the use of TLS certificates of 434 active Booter websites, which allowed us to gain insight into the certificate chain, used cryptography and cipher suites, negotiation protocol, issuer and the validity of the certificate. Our analysis revealed that an increasing number of Booter owners make use of TLS to hide their malicious activities inside encrypted traffic and thus remain undetected by current security tools. Further, we found that Booter websites predominantly use elliptic curve cryptography combined with Galois/Counter mode. We recognized that the TLS certificates of Booter websites often specify numerous SANs. Therefore, we suggest to include the SANs into the Booter blacklist in case they contain certain terms used to describe Booters (e.g., `*stresser*`, `*ddoser*`) as they are most likely also Booter websites.

Acknowledgment

This work was partly supported by the German Federal Ministry of Education and Research (BMBF), the Hessen State Ministry for Higher Education, Research and the Arts (HMWK) within the Center for Research in Security and Privacy (CRISP) and by the Netherlands Organisation for Scientific Research (NWO) Distributed Denial-of-Service Defense: Protecting Schools and other public organizations (D3) Project.

References

[1] Arbor Networks, "Worldwide Infrastructure Security Report," 2015. [Online]. Available from: https://www.arbornetworks.com/images/documents/WISR2016_EN_Web.pdf 2017.05.11

[2] J. Santanna, R. van Rijswijk-Deij, R. Hofstede, A. Sperotto, M. Wierbosch, L. Zambenedetti Granville, and A. Pras, "Booters - An analysis of DDoS-as-a-service attacks," in IFIP/IEEE International Symposium on Integrated Network Management (IM), May 2015, pp. 243–251.

[3] J. Santanna, R. Durban, A. Sperotto, and A. Pras, "Inside booters: An analysis on operational databases," in Integrated Network Management (IM), 2015 IFIP/IEEE International Symposium on, May 2015, pp. 432–440.

[4] J. Steinberger, J. J. Santanna, E. Spatharas, H. Amler, N. Breuer, K. Graul, B. Kuhnert, U. Piontek, A. Sperotto, H. Baier, and A. Pras, ""Ludo" - kids playing Distributed Denial of Service," in TNC16, J. Bergström, G. Hórvath, and B. Schofield, Eds. GÉANT Ltd, November 2016. [Online]. Available from: http://www.eunis.org/erai/2016-2/

[5] Venafi, "Is your SSL Traffic Hiding Attacks?" 2014. [Online]. Available from: https://www.venafi.com/blog/your-ssl-traffic-hiding-attacks 2017.05.11

[6] Dell Inc., "2016 Dell Security Annual Threat Report," 2016. [Online]. Available from: https://www.sonicwall.com/whitepaper/2016-dell-security-annual-threat-report8107907 2017.05.11

[7] E. Gerck, "Overview of Certification Systems: X.509, PKIX, CA, PGP & SKIP," 2000. [Online]. Available from: http://nma.com/mcg-mirror/certover.pdf 2017.05.11

[8] "Booter (black)List." [Online]. Available from: http://booterblacklist.com 2017.06.13

[9] T. Dierks and E. Rescorla, "The Transport Layer Security (TLS) Protocol Version 1.2," RFC 5246 (Proposed Standard), Internet Engineering Task Force, Aug. 2008. [Online]. Available from: http://www.ietf.org/rfc/rfc5246.txt 2017.05.11

[10] D. Eastlake 3rd, "Transport Layer Security (TLS) Extensions: Extension Definitions," RFC 6066 (Proposed Standard), Internet Engineering Task Force, Jan. 2011. [Online]. Available from: http://www.ietf.org/rfc/rfc6066.txt 2017.05.11

[11] D. Cooper, S. Santesson, S. Farrell, S. Boeyen, R. Housley, and W. Polk, "Internet X.509 Public Key Infrastructure Certificate and Certificate Revocation List (CRL) Profile," RFC 5280 (Proposed Standard), Internet Engineering Task Force, May 2008. [Online]. Available from: http://www.ietf.org/rfc/rfc5280.txt 2017.05.11
[12] W3Techs, "Usage of SSL certificate authorities for websites," 2016. [Online]. Available from: http://w3techs.com/technologies/overview/ssl_certificate/all 2017.05.11
[13] B. Hein, "PKI Trust Models: Whom do you trust?" 2013. [Online]. Available from: https://www.sans.org/reading-room/whitepapers/vpns/pki-trust-models-trust-36112 2017.05.11
[14] CA/Browser Forum , "EV SSL Certificate Guidelines V1_5_9," 2016. [Online]. Available from: https://cabforum.org/extended-validation 2017.05.11
[15] European Commision, "EU Trusted Lists of Certification Service Providers," 2016. [Online]. Available from: https://ec.europa.eu/digital-single-market/en/eu-trusted-lists-certification-service-providers 2017.05.11
[16] Anonymous, "Comments on the Article of Detecting Certificate Authority compromises and web browser collusion," 2011. [Online]. Available from: https://blog.torproject.org/blog/detecting-certificate-authority-compromises-and-web-browser-collusion 2017.05.11
[17] Comodo Group, Inc, "Secure faxing. Secure e-mail. Secure backup - Anywhere, anytime." 2004. [Online]. Available from: https://www.comodo.com/news/press_releases/12_01_04.html 2017.05.11
[18] Thawte, "About Thawte," 2016. [Online]. Available from: https://www.thawte.com/about/ 2017.05.11
[19] T. Callan, "VeriSign completes acquisition of GeoTrust," 2005. [Online]. Available from: http://www.symantec.com/connect/blogs/verisign-completes-acquisition-geotrust 2017.05.11
[20] I. Grant, "Symantec completes $1.28bn VeriSign acquisition," 2010. [Online]. Available from: http://www.computerweekly.com/news/1280093508/Symantec-completes-128bn-VeriSign-acquisition 2017.05.11
[21] C. Soghoian and S. Stamm, "Certified Lies: Detecting and Defeating Government Interception Attacks Against SSL (Short Paper)," in Proceedings of the 15th International Conference on Financial Cryptography and Data Security, ser. FC'11. Berlin, Heidelberg: Springer-Verlag, 2012, pp. 250–259.
[22] E. Nigg, "Unbelievable!" 2008. [Online]. Available from: https://groups.google.com/forum/#!topic/mozilla.dev.tech.crypto/nAzIKSBEh78%5B1-25%5D 2017.05.11
[23] SSL Shopper, "SSL Certificate for Mozilla.com Issued Without Validation," 2008. [Online]. Available from: https://www.sslshopper.com/article-ssl-certificate-for-mozilla.com-issued-without-validation.html 2017.05.11
[24] Comodo Group, Inc, "Comodo SSL Affiliate - The Recent RA Compromise," 2011. [Online]. Available from: https://blog.comodo.com/other/the-recent-ra-compromise 2017.05.11
[25] Comodo Group, Inc , "Comodo Incident Report," 2011. [Online]. Available from: https://www.comodo.com/Comodo-Fraud-Incident-2011-03-23.html 2017.05.11
[26] DigiNotar Damage Disclosure, "DigiNotar reports security incident," 2011. [Online]. Available from: https://blog.torproject.org/blog/diginotar-damage-disclosure 2017.05.11
[27] VASCO Data Security International, Inc, "DigiNotar reports security incident," 2011. [Online]. Available from: https://www.vasco.com/about-vasco/press/2011/news_diginotar_reports_security_incident.html 2017.05.11
[28] Microsoft Security TechCenter, "Improperly Issued Digital Certificates Could Allow Spoofing," 2015. [Online]. Available from: https://technet.microsoft.com/en-us/library/security/3046310.aspx 2017.05.11
[29] D. Pauli, "Microsoft scrambles to kill Live.fi man-in-the-middle diddle," 2015. [Online]. Available from: http://www.theregister.co.uk/2015/03/17/redmond_scrambles_to_kill_livefi_maninthemiddle_diddle 2017.05.11
[30] E. Rescorla, "HTTP Over TLS," RFC 2818 (Informational), Internet Engineering Task Force, May 2000. [Online]. Available from: http://www.ietf.org/rfc/rfc2818.txt 2017.05.11
[31] S. Alrwais, K. Yuan, E. Alowaisheq, Z. Li, and X. Wang, "Understanding the Dark Side of Domain Parking," in 23rd USENIX Security Symposium (USENIX Security 14). San Diego, CA: USENIX Association, Aug. 2014, pp. 207–222. [Online]. Available from: https://www.usenix.org/conference/usenixsecurity14/technical-sessions/presentation/alrwais 2017.05.11
[32] Z. Li, S. Alrwais, Y. Xie, F. Yu, and X. Wang, "Finding the Linchpins of the Dark Web: a Study on Topologically Dedicated Hosts on Malicious Web Infrastructures," in Security and Privacy (SP), 2013 IEEE Symposium on, May 2013, pp. 112–126.
[33] CA/Browser Forum , "Baseline Requirements Certificate Policy for the Issuance and Management of Publicly-Trusted Certificates Version 1.3.7," 2016. [Online]. Available from: https://cabforum.org/wp-content/uploads/CA-Browser-Forum-BR-1.3.7.pdf 2017.05.11
[34] Y. Liu, W. Tome, L. Zhang, D. Choffnes, D. Levin, B. Maggs, A. Mislove, A. Schulman, and C. Wilson, "An End-to-End Measurement of Certificate Revocation in the Web's PKI," in Proceedings of the 2015 ACM Conference on Internet Measurement Conference, ser. IMC '15. New York, NY, USA: ACM, 2015, pp. 183–196.
[35] "Ciphersuites of TLS Client." [Online]. Available from: https://www.dasec.h-da.de/staff/benjamin-kuhnert 2017.06.13
[36] J. Salowey, A. Choudhury, and D. McGrew, "AES Galois Counter Mode (GCM) Cipher Suites for TLS," RFC 5288 (Proposed Standard), Internet Engineering Task Force, Aug. 2008. [Online]. Available from: http://www.ietf.org/rfc/rfc5288.txt 2017.05.11
[37] E. Rescorla, "TLS Elliptic Curve Cipher Suites with SHA-256/384 and AES Galois Counter Mode (GCM)," RFC 5289 (Informational), Internet Engineering Task Force, Aug. 2008. [Online]. Available from: http://www.ietf.org/rfc/rfc5289.txt 2017.05.11
[38] E. Barker, "Recommendation for Key Management - Part 1: General," 2016. [Online]. Available from: http://nvlpubs.nist.gov/nistpubs/SpecialPublications/NIST.SP.800-57pt1r4.pdf 2017.05.11
[39] N. Sullivan, "ECDSA: The digital signature algorithm of a better internet," 2014. [Online]. Available from: https://blog.cloudflare.com/ecdsa-the-digital-signature-algorithm-of-a-better-internet 2017.05.11
[40] namestat.org , "How many top-level domains are there now? 300? 500? No, it's 1,000," 2016. [Online]. Available from: https://namestat.org/s/gtld-program 2017.05.11
[41] W3Techs, "Comodo has become the most widely used SSL certificate authority," 2016. [Online]. Available from: https://w3techs.com/blog/entry/comodo_has_become_the_most_widely_used_ssl_certificate_authority 2017.05.11
[42] J. Steinberger, A. Sperotto, H. Baier, and A. Pras, "Collaborative attack mitigation and response: A survey," in 2015 IFIP/IEEE International Symposium on Integrated Network Management (IM), May 2015, pp. 910–913.
[43] J. Steinberger, L. Schehlmann, S. Abt, and H. Baier, Anomaly Detection and Mitigation at Internet Scale: A Survey. Berlin, Heidelberg: Springer Berlin Heidelberg, 2013, pp. 49–60.
[44] J. J. Santanna and A. Sperotto, "Characterizing and Mitigating the DDoS-as-a-Service Phenomenon," in Monitoring and Securing Virtualized Networks and Services: 8th IFIP WG 6.6 International Conference on Autonomous Infrastructure, Management, and Security, AIMS 2014, A. Sperotto, G. Doyen, S. Latré, M. Charalambides, and B. Stiller, Eds. Berlin, Heidelberg: Springer Berlin Heidelberg, 2014, pp. 74–78.

Lucene Based Block Indexing Technology on Large Email Data

Chunyao Song, Yao Ge, Peng Nie and Xiaojie Yuan

College of Computer and
Control Engineering
Nankai University
Tianjin, China 300071
Email: {chunyao.song, geyao, niepeng, yuanxj}@nankai.edu.cn

***Abstract*—As a warehouse for storing and managing data, a relational database supports the index mechanism, to meet users' needs of managing data resources. However, when the amount of data is too large or the users' queries are complicated, its simple index structure is not able to return an accurate query result within a short time. Thus, we need to establish a highly efficient index scheme for large amounts of data. Given that the users' primary requirement is searching keywords on a specified batch interval on large email data, where each email is associated with a batch attribute, this work builds an email retrieval system by using a full-text searching toolkit called Lucene. This work presents a scheme to build the index according to each email's batch attribute and achieves the coexistence of the block index and the integrated index. The evaluation shows that our scheme has significantly improved the searching efficiency of the email retrieval system compared to the basic system which does not allow a hybrid index structure.**

Keywords–Lucene; index; email data; big data.

I. Introduction

This is an information and Internet Plus era. The Internet is flooded with plenty of information. How to retrieve the most useful information from the massive data was a main challenge from the very beginning of the development of the Internet. The appearance of searching engine gives us a solution. Searching, as a mainstream method to get useful information, becomes part of people's daily life.

The index structure has determined the response time and query accuracy of a searching engine to a large extent. The index mechanism in a database system is a common scheme. However, the index structure of traditional relational database is very simple, and lacks the core functionality for retrieving and analyzing the contents of the files stored in the library [1]. Although it supports normal SQL (structured query language)-based queries well, it is hard to meet the requirements of a search engine. First of all, a search engine needs to search large amounts of data, and the storage format is relatively simple. How to use a database to reasonably and effectively manage this data is a difficult problem. Second, the demand of a search engine is to give an accurate response within a short time for a large number of users' query requests. Therefore, the time consuming work should be completed during the index building phase. In other words, before run time. Apparently, the index structure in the database system does not meet this need. Therefore, it is necessary to establish an efficient index library for massive data.

Lucene is a subproject of the Apache software foundation [2]. It is an open source java-based full-text search engine architecture. It provides a complete query engine, index engine and part of the text analysis engine [3]-[4]. Thus, software developers can easily achieve full-text search function in the target system. As an excellent full-text search engine architecture, Lucene has greatly improved the retrieval efficiency, by using highly optimized inverted index structure [5]. A main advantage of Lucene is that the format of the indexed file is independent of the application platform. It defines a set of 8-bytes-based index file formats so that compatible systems or applications of different platforms can share the establishment of the index file [6]-[7].

The full-text retrieval system is a software system, aiming to provide full-text retrieval services based on full-text search theory. There are two parts to complete full-text search. One is to build and maintain the index library. The other is an efficient and accurate retrieval mechanism. Lucene has provided calling interfaces for both parts. However, in practical applications, Lucene has a problem that should be noticed. The size of the index file is linearly increasing as the number of files needing to be indexed increases. When the primary requirement is to do interval filter for a specific field first, and then do keyword search, whether the search engine needs to search the entire index file every time is worth studying. Based on this, we propose a scheme to create a block index based on this field. We split the GigaByte-level index file into multiple small index files according to this field. Then, we only need to search on small index files which satisfy the query range and merge the search results during the searching phase.

When an index file reaches the GigaByte-level, for a single server, if the filter interval given by the query is small, then the block index may significantly improve the searching speed. However, when the range of the filter field in the query is large, integrated index may perform better than block index during the searching phase. As using block index needs to read multiple index files, there is a need for frequent I/O (Input/Output) operations. As a conclusion, choosing different index scheme according to different search situations may improve the average response time of the search engine as a whole.

The target searching dataset for this work is a large email dataset. Each email contains an eight-digit batch attribute. The primary user requirement is to search for a specified keyword within some batch of messages. Therefore, it is of great significance to improve the search efficiency by implementing the full-text search system which realizes coexistence of the block index and the integrated index. It is very meaningful to improve the search efficiency for different search requests.

Given the email dataset stored in MySQL - a commercial relational database management system [8], the idea of this work is to create a block index and an integrated index for each attribute of each record/email. The search function is completed based on the establishement of the index file. Thus, the user could query the system. After the basic structure of the email retrieval system is completed, the optimization by using block index is introduced. Evaluation is performed to help choose the appropriate indexing strategy based on users' searching needs. Finally, the strategy is used to improve the searching efficiency of the email retrieval system.

In the remainder of this paper, we first give a brief introduction about Lucene [2] in Section II. We will introduce the index engine and search engine of Lucene. Next, we will show our system design method and implementation details in Section III. We will explain in details how to accomplish the index building for our email retrieval system, and how to perform the searching process based on the established index. Evaluation results is shown in Section IV. We perform comprehensive experiments to select the best index strategy for different searching requirement. Section V gives the conclusion of the paper.

II. PRELIMINARIES— A REVIEW OF LUCENE THEORY

Lucene consists of eight packages, each of which is invoked with other packets. They have specific functions, such as text analysis, index creating, index read-write, index structure management, and search requests parsing, etc. [9]. Lucene works by converting other data formats into text, extracting the index entries and related information from the word breaker, and then writing the information to the index file, and saving it to disk or memory. We will introduce Lucene theory from both the index engine and the search engine.

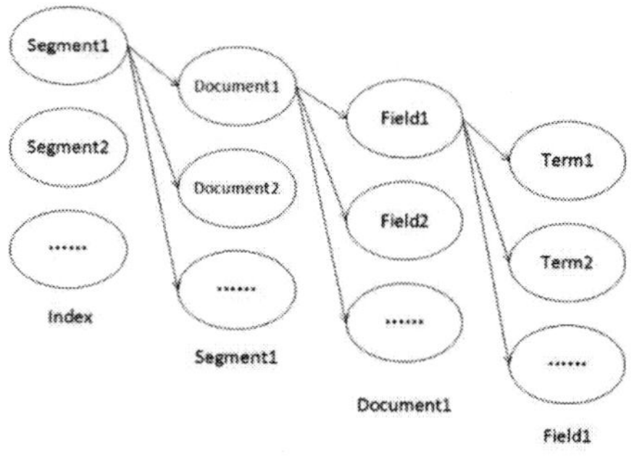

Figure 1. Lucene Index Conceptual Relationship

A. Lucene's Index Engine

There are five basic concepts in Lucene, including **Index**, **Document**, **Field**, **Term** and **Segment**. The relationships are shown in Figure 1.

- An **index** consists of multiple documents.
- A **document** consists of multiple files. It is similar to a record in relational database, which is mainly responsible for domain management [10].
- A **field** consists of several terms. Each field usually has four attributes: name of the field, value of the field, whether it is necessary to be stored in index file and whether it is indexed.
- A **term** is a string that is obtained by lexical analysis and language processing of the text, which is the searching unit. It has two attributes: the name of the term and the value of the term.
- A **segment** can be considered as a tiny index. It includes all documents needed by the index. When adding new documents to the index being searched, Lucene usually creates a new segment to avoid the cost of rebuilding the index.

When creating an index, it is not that every record is immediately added to the same index file. They are first written to a different small file, and then merged into a large index file [11]. The source provided by the user is a record in the database table. A record is indexed and then stored in the index file.

Lucene holds only one buffer when building index. However, it provides three parameters to adjust the size of the buffer and the frequency to write the index file to disk [2]. These three parameters are:

- **Merge factor**: this parameter controls the timing of merging index files on a disk into large index files and the number of documents that can be stored in each index block.
- **Minimum number of merged documents**: this parameter is the minimum value that the number of documents in memory want to write to disk. If there is enough memory, increasing this parameter could significantly improve the index efficiency.
- **Maximum number of merged documents**: this parameter is the maximum number of documents an index block can store. Appropriate increase in this parameter value can speed up the index building process and shorten the response time.

B. Lucene's Search Engine

Lucene supports a variety of query methods. Combining them allows developers to customize the queriers needed. We need three kinds of queries in this work.

- **TermQuery**: it allows to search for keywords for specified field.
- **BooleanQuery**: it supports query combination. By adding a variety of query objects and designating their logical relationship as "and", "or", "non", it can link the queries together.
- **RangeQuery**: it supports range search on a specific field. It can also be used together with BooleanQuery.

Based on this search engine, the searching process includes five steps. The first step is to read the index file. Lucene provides an IndexReader. After its open() method has been invoked, it will find the latest segment from the index file. It will load the meta data of this segment into memory, and further open each segment and the documents within each segment.

The second step is to build the search tree. Given the structure of the query object, Lucene will parse it into a query tree based on the logic of the query. When multiple search conditions are used, Boolean queries are usually used as logical join queries. In this case, a Boolean query can be used to represent the entire query tree.

The third step is to evaluate the weight. Weight is the factor used to calculate the score. When the query tree is obtained, the first operation is to rewrite the query tree. The purpose is to change the query tree according to the need of searching keywords change. Then, use the recursive creation of the weight tree based on the newly obtained query tree, and calculate the value of the public part of each document in the scoring formula.

The fourth step is to calculate the document score. The matching is performed by calculating the similarity between the query and the document. Each search result will be given a score. The higher the score, the higher the degree of matching. The scoring function is the **score** method in class **Scorer**. It traverses all the resulting documents to calculate the score. The scoring mechanism it used is the TF/IDF (Term Frequency/Inverse Document Frequency) [12] algorithm. The tf-idf weight is a weight often used in information retrieval and text mining. This weight is a statistical measure used to evaluate how important a word is to a document in a collection or corpus. We have discussed in index engine that the documents are divided into words when creating an index. Word segmentation is also performed in the searching phase. TF/IDF algorithm considers how many times the word appears and how many words appear in the document. The TF frequency of the keyword is calculated as follows: $tf_{i,j} = \frac{n_{i,j}}{\sum_k n_{k,j}}$ [12], where $n_{i,j}$ is the number of occurrences of the keyword in the document d_j, and $\sum_k n_{k,j}$ is the summation of the number of occurrences of all keywords in document d_j. For a specific document, the greater the proportion of the number of occurrences of a keyword to the number of occurrences of all keywords, the stronger the ability of this keyword to distinguish between the attributes of the document, and the greater the value of the calculated TF value [13]. The IDF value is computed as $idf_i = \frac{|D|}{|\{d:d \in t_i\}|}$ [12], where $|D|$ is the total number of documents, and $|\{d : d \in t_i\}|$ is the number of documents which contains the keyword t_i. The greater the number of documents that contain a keyword in the document set, the weaker the ability of the keyword to distinguish the attributes of the document category, resulting in a smaller corresponding IDF weight. Finally, the TF-IDF is computed as $(tf - idf)_{i,j} = tf_{i,j} * idf_i$ [12]. The resulting score reflects the ability of a keyword to reflect the document subject. The larger the final score, the better the effect of the keyword that reflects the subject of the document. The document score is computed as the summation of the score of each word segmentation term. A priority queue is used to store the resulting documents, which has a sorting function at the same time.

The last step is to return the query result. After computing the score of each searched document, Lucene will return the query results in decreasing order.

III. System Design and Implementation

The email retrieval system of this work is implemented based on JavaWeb [14] and Lucene. We have introduced the theory of index building and query processing in previous sections. We will discuss how to build the index of a dataset based on the interfaces Lucene provides, and how to accept users' searching queries and return the searching results based on JavaWeb in this section.

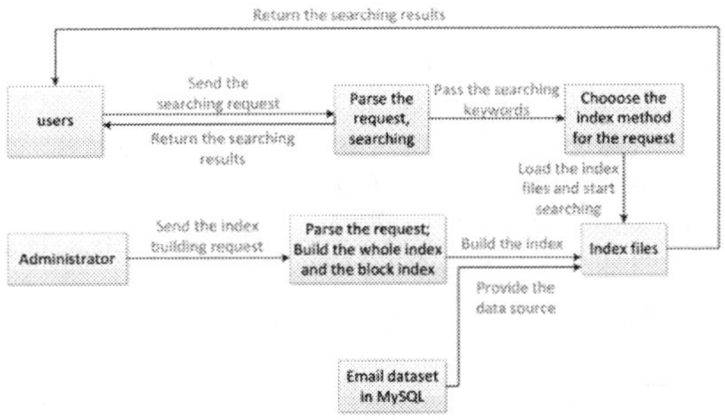

Figure 2. System Design Flow Chart

The system design flow chart is shown in Figure 2. As we are trying to develop an email retrieval system, the datset we use is an email dataset. The emails have already been parsed based on receiver, sender, copy recipients, email contents, etc., and stored in MySQL. Each email has an eight digits batch label, so that users could search on specified batches. Since users have a great need to search keywords on emails with specified batches, we build two kinds of indexes for the input dataset:

- **Integrated index**: this kind of index builds index for each attribute of the email, and finally there is only one index files folder, which includes all index files needed for query processing.
- **Block index**: the blocks are divided according to the batch label of each email. We build an index files folder for each batch of the emails. The name of the index files folder is the batch name and the number of the index files folders equals the number of email batches.

After finishing the index building, the user could launch the searching request according to personal needs. The system server then decides which index method to use according to the specific request. Based on this, the server then loads the index files for searching and returns the search results.

A. *Index Building*

Index building is an important part of system implementation. Before we build the index, we need to confirm how to do the word segmentation for the documents awaited to be analyzed, which information should be stored for future use, and which fields will be used for future queries. We will introduce how to build integrated index and block index based on relevant kernel classes and the call graph. Figure 3 shows the kernel classes needed for index building and the call graph.

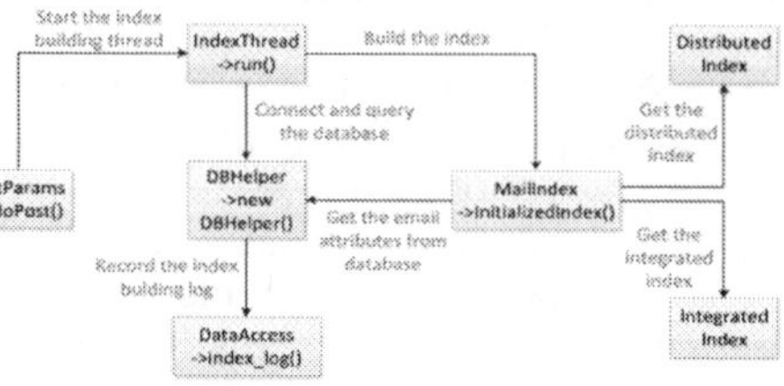

Figure 3. Kernel Classes Needed for Index Building and the Call Graph

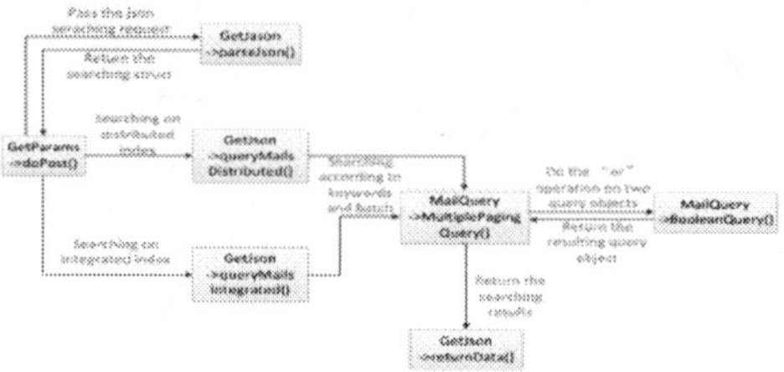

Figure 4. Kernel Classes Needed for Searching Process and the Call Graph

- Class **GetParams**: this class is inherited from HttpServlet. After the doPost() function of this class receives the request for index building, it will create an object of class IndexThread. It will then call the start() method of IndexThread to start the thread, and start the index building.
- Class **IndexThread**: because the data are stored in MySQL, after the thread is started, the run() method of this class will first load all batch information from the database. It will then create index file folder according to the information and name each index file using the corresponding batch name. After that, it will pass the file folder path and the current batch information to the InitializeIndex() method of the MailIndex class. If we are building integrated index, then the passed batch information is a null string. So, we could build the two kinds of indexes at the same time.
- Class **MailIndex**: since our email retrieval system needs to do full-text search, the InitializeIndex() method of this class will create an object of the DBHelper class, to connect to the MySQL database, read all attributes of the dataset, and build the index based on the interfaces Lucene provides. This method accepts two parameters, which are index building path and the email batch information.
- Class **DBHelper**: the simplest nonparametric constructor function of this class is able to connect to the database. The one-parametric constructor adds a function to get ready to execute the statement.

Since we need to build the block index at the same time when we build the integrated index, we use one parameter of the InitializeIndex() method to accept the email batch. After receiving the email batch needed for index building, we use JDBC (Java Database Connectivity) [15] to connect to MySQL, and select all emails which have this specified batch, and then create an IndexWriter object of Lucene to build the index.

B. Searching Process

The searching process includes parsing the search request, opening the index files for searching, and returning the searching results to users. We will show the call graph according to these three steps and explain the details. Figure 4 shows the call graph.

- Class **GetParams**: users send the post request to JavaWeb server using browser. The searching request is passed by json. In the meanwhile, http request is acquired and encapsulated by Servlet container to the HttpServlet object. The doPost() method of this class is responsible for receiving the searching request, and passing the json string to the GetJson object created. It will call the GetJson methods for future parsing, querying, and results returning.
- Class **GetJson**: the parseJson() method of this class is responsible for parsing the json string, and generate the searching structure. It has two parameters. The first is the json string for the searching request. The second is whether should use the block index to parse the searching request. The generated searching structure is returned to GetParams. After receive the searching structure, GetParams would call different GetJson methods for integrated index and block index. The block index will call queryMailsDistributed() method, which needs to do searching on every index file within this batch, while integrated index will call queryMailsIntegrated() method, which only does searching on the single index file. These two methods will both call MultiplePagingQuery() method of MailQuery.
When accepting the request, the relevant information is received. Thus, after getting the searching results, the returnData() method of this class will call the relevant methods, to generate the response data and pass the response to the user.
- Class **MailQuery**: this class will do searching according to the received request. The MultiplePagingQuery() method and the BooleanQuery() methods are two kernel methods.

After receiving the searching keywords and the batch information, the system will use QueryParser in MultiplePagingQuery() to construct the searching object according to the keywords. It will use BooleanQuery to do the "or" operation on the two searching objects: one is the QueryParser of the keywords, while the other is the RangeQuery of the batch. Further, it will use IndexReader and IndexSearcher to open the index, and perform the searching process.

IV. EVALUATION

We have discussed how to build the two kinds of indexes, how to perform the searching process and how to return the results. However, we are still not sure when to use which kind of index under what scenario. Thus, we need to do the searching evaluation. We will discuss the design of the

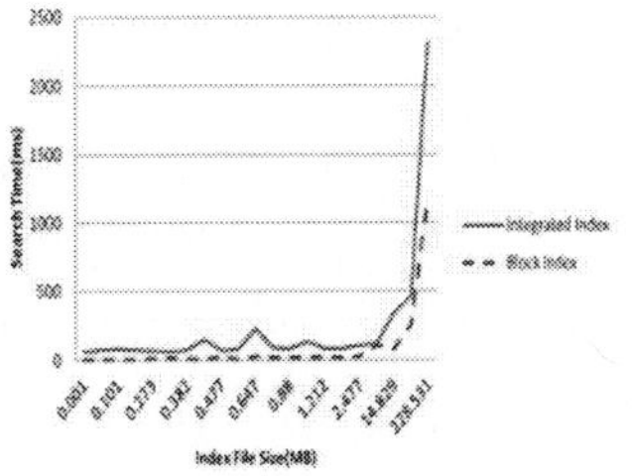

Figure 5. Partial index files searching time comparison

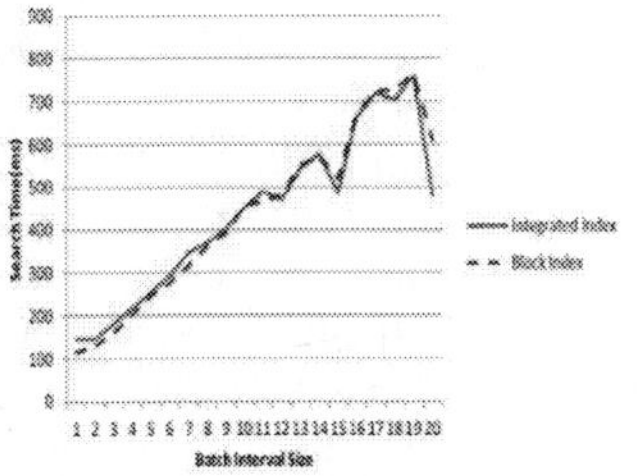

Figure 6. Searching time comparison for batch interval in 1-20

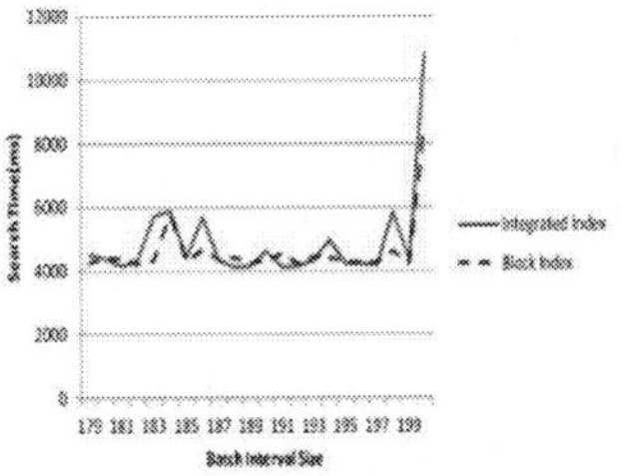

Figure 7. Searching time comparison for batch interval in 179-200

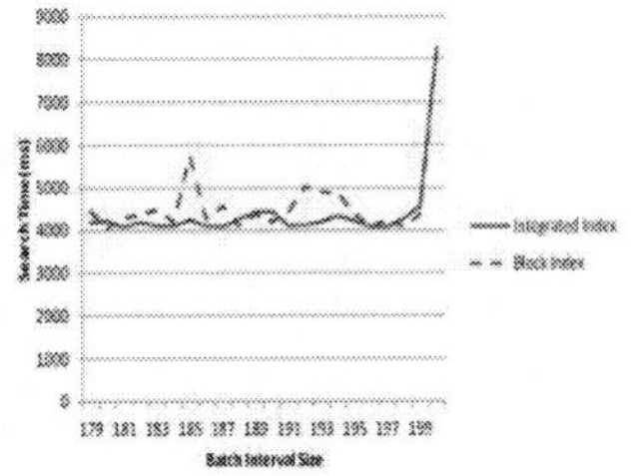

Figure 8. Searching time comparison for exchangeable search and batch interval in 179-200

searching evaluation, searching results analysis and searching strategy development based on experimental results in this section.

A. Evaluation Design and Implementation

The batch interval decides how many block index files needed to be loaded into the disk. The size of a block index depends on the amount of data needed to be loaded into the memory. Different keywords will result in different sizes of result sets. They will all affect the searching efficiency. Thus, we perform the experiments by varing parameters from these three aspects.

The searching evaluation uses URL and URLConnection classes of Java [16] to send searching requests to Class GetParams. In order to get the statistics of the searching time conveniently, we modify the searching code so the server only return the searching time, instead of returning the searching results. We then output the returning searching time directly to an excel file, and finally get the statistics for analysis.

B. Evaluation Results and Analysis

The effect of the size of index file: since the number of emails in different batches is different, and the size of each block index file is different, in order to evaluate the effect of the size of index file to searching efficiency, we need to search on each batch. The partial average result is shown in Table I.

TABLE I. THE EFFECT OF SIZE OF INDEX FILE TO SEARCHING EFFICIENCY

size of index file(MB)	block index time(s)	integrated index time
0.001	0.006	0.061
0.406	0.009	0.073
1.107	0.012	0.077
4.157	0.034	0.109
22.015	0.123	0.260
51.934	0.254	0.463
94.237	0.372	0.880
228.368	1.250	2.208

We perform the searching evaluation on 200 batches. We show partial results according to certain interval for clarity. The comparison of integrated index and block index is shown in Figure 5. We can see from the experimental results that when we search on one batch, block index is obviously better than integrated index. The smaller the index file, the more apparent difference between the two methods. When the size of the index file is less than 1MB, the searching efficiency of block index is 10 times better than integrated index. As the size of the index file increases, the advantage of the block index is decreases.

The effect of the batch interval: We have seen from the previous test that when the batch interval is 1, the block index has significant advantages. However, as the batch interval is increasing, the I/O cost of block index is increasing as well. So the advantage is expected to decrease. So, the assumption is there is a cross point that before this point, the block index is better than integrated index. While after this point, the integrated index is better than block index. We perform the experiments on 200 batches, and extend the batch interval from 1 to 200 gradually. The partial average searching time is shown in Table II.

TABLE II. THE EFFECT OF SIZE OF SEARCHING BATCH INTERVAL

size of batch interval	average block index searching time (s)	average integrated index searching time (s)
1	0.115	0.146
10	0.391	0.399
20	0.765	0.756
50	1.699	1.621
90	2.846	2.769
140	4.613	4.152
200	8.590	10.811

Because it is hard to present the 200 test results in a single figure, we show the first part of the results in Figure 6. We can see that block index is better than integrated index when batch interval is less than 11. It means that when users' searching request includes less than 11 batches, we should use block index. The integrated index performs better than block index in the middle part.

However, the last experiments did not perform as expected. In our expectation, since the block index needs to load multiple index file folders to memory, the frequent I/O operation becomes the bottleneck. Thus, the searching efficiency should be worse than integrated index. However, as we seen in Figure 7, the block index performs close to or even better than integrated index in most cases. Since we did the experiments on block index and integrated index respectively, it is possible that the system did not do the whole I/O operations in every searching. Thus, we perform experiments for block index and integrated index alternatively. The result is shown in Figure 8. We can see that in this case the integrated index performs better than block index. So, we should still use integrated index when the batch interval is large.

The effect of the size of the results set: Under the single server environment, the searching results are stored in the Java stack. When the size of the returning results is large, continuous searching will result in high memory usage. This will further affect the data exchange between disk and memory, resulting in low searching efficiency.

We perform a test on the effect of different keywords and the results are similar to previous experiments, thus we omit the figure here. The cross point of graph appears in the range 10 to 15. It means the search efficiency of block index and integrated index is equal when the size of batch interval is 10 to 15. In other words, block index performs better in small batch interval, while integrated index performs better in large batch interval.

C. Searching Strategy Development

We can see from the experimental results, when the batch interval is less than 10, the searching efficiency of block index is better than the integrated index in most cases. However, when the batch interval is large, say, approching 200, the searching efficiency of integrated index is better than block index. When the batch interval is in the middle, the searching efficiency of the two methods are close. However, due to the uncertainty of searching request, there could be great differences among the two continuous searching requests. Thus, to reduce the disk I/O operation, it is recommended to use integrated index.

Moreover, considering a large batch will decrease the searching efficiency of block index, we could record the large batches in advance. When the searching request touches on many those batches, we could use integrated index.

V. CONCLUSIONS AND FUTURE WORK

Compared to the traditional SQL language, Lucene has unbeatable searching efficiency. It provides friendly interfaces and clear documentation. So, the software engineer could develop a search engine in a short time. However, when the amount of data increases sharply, the linear increase of the size of the index files lowers the efficiency of searching within a specific range.

Our system focuses on a specific email dataset. We need to satisfy the requirement to searching keywords within some specific batches. So, we need to realize the function for fast search under multiple restrictions. We propose to divide the index files according to batch labels, in other words, block index. We develop the system based on JavaWeb [17] and Lucene. We implemented both integrated index and block index, to accpet the user requests and return the results to users. In order to decide the index using strategy, we perform comprehensive searching experiments, considering the problem from three aspects: the size of a index file, the searching batch interval, and the keywords differential. We develop a meaningful method to compute the average searching time. We perform comprehensive experiments and the evaluation results show our scheme has significantly improved the searching efficiency of the email retrieval system compared to the basic system which does not allow hybrid index structure. We compare the searching efficiency using both tables and figures, and show the strategy at the end. We have reduced the users' waiting time while at the same time when satisfying users' requirement.

Although the block index has increased the efficiency to some extent, we could still improve in some aspects. Currently, we only use the batch interval to select different index methods. We could consider more factors for choosing the index methods. When there are lots of searching results, it will occupy a lot of memory so the searching efficiency will decrease. We could try better results returning methods. We use single machine in this work. However, when the data size further increases, we could try to deploy the system in a distributed manner. In that case, how to merge the searching results and do the scoring is another problem worth considering.

ACKNOWLEDGMENT

This work was supported in part by Natural Science Foundation of Tianjin, under Grant No. 17JCYBJC23800; National 863 Program of China, under Grant No. 2015AA015401; and Research Foundation of The Ministry of Education and China Mobile, under Grant No. MCM20150507. Chunyao Song and Yao Ge contribute equally to this work.

REFERENCES

[1] Y. Xu, Y. Zhu, C. Li, and W. Wang, "The design and implementation of lucene based full-text retrieval on massive database," *Journal of Hunan University of Technology*, vol. 25(2), pp. 81–84, 2011.

[2] Lucene. http://lucene.apache.org/. [accessed: 2017-06-06].

[3] K. Yang, X. Shi, and E. Tang, "Reptile based software defects prediction," *Journal of Nanchang College of Education*, vol. 31(6), pp. 125–128, 2016.

[4] J. Zhang and J. Wang, "Discussion about the integration of lucene in haobai searching engine," *Science & Technology Information*, vol. (21), pp. 12–12, 2012.

[5] H. Tang, Y. He, X. Xu, and C. Xu, "Lucene based distributed parallel index," *Computer Technology and Development*, vol. 21(2), pp. 123–126, 2011.

[6] H. Wu, "Lucene based email forensics technology," *Netinfo Security*, vol. 10, pp. 181–184, 2013.

[7] L. Yuan, "Discussion about the functions and applications of lucene based full-text index," *Science and Technology of West China*, vol. 11(5), pp. 37–38, 2012.

[8] https://www.mysql.com/. [accessed: 2017-06-06].

[9] X. Shi and Z. Wang, "An optimized full-text retrieval system based on lucene in oracle database," *Enterprise System Conference*, pp. 61–65, 2014.

[10] R. Gao, D. Li, W. Li, and Y. Dong, "Application of full text search engine based on lucene," *Advances in Internet of Things*, vol. 02(4), pp. 106–109, 2012.

[11] S. Yue, W. Li, L. Wang, and S. Guang, "Index for database retrieval based on lucene," *Journal of Jilin University (Science Edition)*, vol. (5), pp. 995–1000, 2014.

[12] A. Rajaraman and J. Ullman, "Miing of massaive datasets," pp. 1–17, 2011.

[13] X. Wang and G. Ren, "An improved wpr algorithm based on the most recent searching period's referencing frequency," *Computer Science*, vol. 43(2), pp. 86–88, 2016.

[14] http://docs.oracle.com/javase/tutorial/deployment/webstart/. [accessed: 2017-06-07].

[15] https://docs.oracle.com/javase/8/docs/technotes/guides/jdbc/. [accessed: 2017-06-06].

[16] https://www.java.com. [accessed: 2017-06-07].

[17] http://www.vogella.com/tutorials/javawebterminology/article.html. [accessed: 2017-06-06].

An Efficient Reachability Queries Approach for Large Graph based on Cluster Structure

Yale Chai, Yao Ge
Chunyao Song and Peng Nie

College of Computer and Control Engineering, Nankai University
38 Tongyan Road, Tianjin 300350, P.R.China
Email: {chaiyl, geyao}@dbis.nankai.edu.cn, {chunyao.song, niepeng}@nankai.edu.cn

***Abstract*—Reachability query is a fundamental operation on graphs that finds the connection between vertices. Although plenty of techniques have been proposed for reachability queries, most of them are designed for directed graphs. Existing techniques for undirected graphs cannot handle large volumes of data. In this paper, we propose an undirected graph reachability (UGR) query algorithm by integrating graph clustering algorithm with traditional search methods. We first find core vertices by partitioning them into clusters, and then cluster non-core vertices according to their adjacent core vertices. After clustering, we take each cluster as a new vertex and compute transitive closure. Experimental results demonstrate the effectiveness and scalability of the proposed methods for the reachability query problem.**

Keywords–Reachability queries; Graph cluster; Search method.

I. Introduction

Many real-world networks can be modeled as a graph $G = (V, E)$, where vertices in V represent entities and edges in E represent relationships between entities. Given two vertices u and v, a reachability query asks whether there exists a path between u and v in G. Nowadays, there are lots of techniques for reachability queries on a directed graph. Specifically, for any two vertices u and v in directed graph G, if $u \rightarrow v$ then there exists an order o and $o(u) < o(v)$ [1]. This order will become a vital part to construct the reachability index. As a result, these methods cannot be applied to undirected graphs, due to the non-ordering of undirected vertices. However, many networks can be modeled as undirected graphs. Take the social network for an example, we can treat each user as a vertex and consider the communicating between users as an edge. In this paper, we present a novel study on reachability queries for undirected graphs.

As explained in [2], to answer reachability queries in O(1) time, an extreme practice is to pre-compute and store the full transitive closure of edges, which requires a quadratic space complexity, making it infeasible to handle very large graphs. Our target is to improve the ability to scale to large graphs, as well as reduce the processing time. At present, a trend in dealing with big data is parallel processing: dividing the original data into small pieces, then, separately processing each piece and merging at the end. By clustering graph, we can divide the original graph into "pieces". Among all the graph clustering techniques, the structural graph clustering method can not only cluster graph rather quickly, but also ensure that vertices are reachable to each other within the same cluster. As far as we know, pSCAN [3] is a state-of-art graph clustering approach. Therefore, we propose a method which combing pSCAN with traditional search methods.

The rest of the paper is organized as following: in Section II, we introduce the undirected graph reachability (UGR) query algorithm. In Section III, we conduct complexity analysis, and present the evaluation results. We show the conclusion of our work in Section IV.

II. Our Approach

Based on structural graph clustering, we present UGR approach for reachability querying. Our goal is to scale down the graph before using traditional, full search method. The pseudocode of UGR is shown in Algorithm 1.

Algorithm 1 UGR

Input: A graph $G = (V, E)$), and parameters add $0 < \epsilon < 1$ and $\mu \geq 2$
Output: A new graph $\widetilde{G} = (\widetilde{V}, \widetilde{E})$

Initialize a disjoint-set data structure with vertices in V;
for each vertex $u \in V$ **do**
  core(u) $\leftarrow$ false;
  sd(u) $\leftarrow$ 0 and ed(u) $\leftarrow$ d[u];
end for
for each vertex $u \in V$ in no-increasing order **do**
  Check if u is a core vertex;
  if sd(u)$\geq \mu$ **then**
    core(u) $\leftarrow$ true;
    for each core vertex $v \in N[u]$ **do**
      union(u,v); /* Make u,v in the same cluster */
    end for
  end if
end for
$\mathcal{C}_c \leftarrow$ set of subsets of core vertices;
$\mathcal{C} \leftarrow$ ClusterNoncore(); /* Cluster non-core vertices */
for each cluster $C \in \mathcal{C}$ **do**
  Add a vertex to $\widetilde{V}$;
  Add an edge to $\widetilde{E}$ for each neighbor of C;
end for
Depth-First-Search($\widetilde{G}$);
return $\widetilde{G}$;

Our algorithm mainly contains three steps. Firstly, we divide the graph G into clusters. Secondly, we generate a new graph $\widetilde{G}$ in which each vertex was a cluster in G. Finally, we compute the transitive closures of all vertices in $\widetilde{G}$. As shown in Algorithm 1, we use a disjoint-set data structure which maintains disjoint dynamic subsets. Initially, each vertex forms a singleton subset (Line 1); and the subsets union when vertices in the same cluster. For each vertex $u \in V$, we set u as non-core vertex, at the meantime, we incrementally maintain an effective-degree $ed(u)$ and a similar-degree $sd(u)$ for u (Line 2-5).

We structural cluster graph through a Two-Step Paradigm [3]: cluster core vertices (Line 6-15) and then cluster non-core vertices (line 16). For each vertex v adjacent to u, we compute the structural similarity $\sigma(u,v)$ between u and v as equation 1. If $\sigma(u,v) \geq \epsilon$, then we decide vertex u and v are structural similarity, and increase $sd(u)$ by one. Otherwise, we decrease $ed(u)$ by one. Once $sd(u) \geq \mu$, we determine u as a core vertex. On the contrary, once $ed(u) < \mu$, we determine u as a non-core vertex. In this way, the algorithm can terminate early without visiting all the neighbor of u. Furthermore, if v is a core vertex then we assign u and v to be in the same cluster (line 11).

$$\sigma(u,v) = \frac{|N[u] \bigcap N[v]|}{\sqrt{d[u] \cdot d[v]}} \quad (1)$$

where $N[u]$ is the structural neighborhood of a vertex u, and $d[u]$ is the degree of u.

Algorithm 2 ClusterNoncore

```
1: visited(u) ← false for every vertex;
2: C ← ∅
3: for each cluster C̃ ∈ C_c do
4:    for each vertex u ∈ C̃ do
5:       visited(u) ← true;
6:       for each vertex v ∈ N[u] do
7:          if sd(u)< μ and v ∉ C̃ then
8:             C̃ ← C̃ ∪ {v} /* Add non-core to its neighbor*/
9:             visited(v) ← true;
10:         end if
11:      end for
12:   end for
13: end for
14: /* Handle vertices that belong to no cluster */
15: for each vertex u ∈ G do
16:    if !visited(u) then
17:       Depth-First-Search(u);
18:    end if
19: end for
```

Then, we cluster the rest of the vertices as shown in Algorithm 2. Initially, for each vertex u, we set $visited(u)$ to be false. Given the core cluster $\widetilde{C}$ in C_c, for every vertex $u \in \widetilde{C}$, we include all neighbor of u into the same cluster as $\widetilde{C}$, and mark u,v visited (line 3-13). Obviously, $visited(u)$ equals true means vertex u has been assigned to cluster and no need to be visited in depth-first search (DFS). Afterwards, we iterate through every vertex in G that has not been included to any cluster, and execute DFS to merge it with its neighbor (line 15-19). So far, graph G has been divided into self-connectivity clusters.

Theorem 1: (Internal Connectivity) *Let C be any of clusters of graph G, for any two vertices $v1$, $v2 \in C$, $v1$, $v2$ can reach to each other.*

Proof: As proved in [3], for any two vertices $v1$, $v2 \in C$, there is a vertex $u \in C$ such that both $v1$ and $v2$ are structure-reachable from u. In other words, $v1$ and $v2$ can reach each other within C. ■

In order to compute the transitive closures between clusters, we consider each cluster as a vertex for convenience. The pseudocode to generate a new graph $\widetilde{G}$ is (Algorithm 1 line 17-20): given an empty graph $\widetilde{G}$, we add every cluster C into $\widetilde{G}$ as a vertex. Given two clusters $C1$, $C2$ (new vertex $V1, V2 \in \widetilde{G}$), if there exist an edge between vertex $u \in C1$ and $v \in C2$, then add an new edge between $V1$ and $V2$.

Finally, we use DFS on new graph $\widetilde{G}$ to compute the transitive closures. After that, for any vertex $V \in \widetilde{G}$, we can be aware of the set of vertices that V can reach. At query time, given two vertex $v1, v2 \in G$, we first trace back to their clusters and check the connectivity. The whole query time complexity is $O(1)$.

III. Result Discussion

Theorem 2: (Complexity Analysis) *Given graph G, let $Es \subseteq E$ be the set of adjacent vertex-pairs whose structural similarities have been computed, let N_c be the number of clusters in G. And n, m respectively are the number of vertices and edges in G. The time complexity of our UGR approach is* $O(a(n) \cdot m + \sum_{(u,v)\in Es} min(d[u], d[v]) + N_c^2)$, the space complexity is the $O(m+n)$.

Proof: The first part of the time complexity is related to disjoint-set data structure operations, where $a(n)$ is the extremely slowly growing inverse of the single-valued Ackermann function and is less than 5 for practical values of n. The second part of the time complexity is related to structural similarity computations. As proved in [4], $O(\sum_{(u,v)\in E} min(d[u], d[v])) \leq m^{1.5}$. So, the worst case time complexity of this part is $O(m^{1.5})$. Moreover, we execute DFS on new graph $\widetilde{G}$ who has N_c vertices and at most N_c edges, the second part of the time complexity is $O(N_c^2)$. Normally, the time of this part is so little that can be ignored. Thus, the time complexity of our approach is approximately equal to $O(a(n) \cdot m + O(m^{1.5})$. Besides, the space complexity of UGR is the same as pSCAN [3]. ■

In order to demonstrate our analysis, we implemented our UGR method, and compared it with traditional search methods: *DFS* [5] and *Warshall* [6]. We ran all experiments on a computer with an Intel 3.4 GHz CPU, 16GB RAM, and Windows10 OS. We evaluated the algorithms on five real datasets from the Stanford Network Analysis Platform[1], Table 1 lists the number of vertices and edges in the graphs. Table 2 reports the construction time of process (in ms). We only evaluated the performance of Warshall on first three datasets because it obviously slower than others. What's more, when the scale of dataset is small, DFS had better performance. However, it ran into stack overflow on the last two large graphs. Experiments showed that UGR is more scalable and stable than traditional search methods, especially on sparse graph.

IV. Conclusion and Future Work

This paper presents a study on reachability queries on large undirect graphs, moreover, the thought is easy to extend to the

[1] http://snap.stanford.edu/

TABLE I. DATASETS

DataSet	$\|V\|$	$\|E\|$
CA-GrQc	5242	14496
Enron	13220	111467
Cit-HepTh	27770	352,807
Email-EuAll	265,214	420,045
DBLP	317,080	1,049,866

TABLE II. COMPARISON OF CONSTRUCTION TIME

DataSet	*Warshall*	*DFS*	*UGR*
Enron(10000 mails)	4663	2	11
Enron(30000 mails)	73277	18	38
Enron(50000 mails)	651981	17	74
Enron(all)	–	23	107
CA-GrQc	–	28	7
Cit-HepTh	–	132	380
Email-EuAll	–	–	388
dblp	–	–	1064

directed graph as long as we change the clustering method. Based on the experiments, we show that our algorithms is more scalable and stable than traditional search methods, especially on sparse graph. For future work, this work can be extended in several interesting directions. First, we will study the evaluation of graph shortest-path search queries. Second, we will improve the clustering method and make our approach applied to the weighted graph. Third, we will exploit the distributed database to achieve higher scalability in terms of graph sizes.

ACKNOWLEDGMENT

This work was supported in part by Natural Science Foundation of Tianjin, under Grant No. 17JCYBJC23800; National 863 Program of China, under Grant No. 2015AA015401; and Research Foundation of The Ministry of Education and China Mobile, under Grant No. MCM20150507.

REFERENCES

[1] A. D. Zhu, W. Lin, S. Wang, and X. Xiao, "Reachability Queries on Large Dynamic Graphs: A Total Order Approach," in *Proceedings of the 2014 ACM SIGMOD International Conference on Management of Data June 22-27, 2014, Snowbird, Utah, USA*, pp. 1323–1334, ISBN: 978-1-4503-2376-5.

[2] Y. Hilmi, V. Chaoji, and M. J. Zaki, "GRAIL: scalable reachability index for large graphs," *Proceedings of the VLDB Endowment*, vol. 3(1), pp. 276–284, 2010, ISSN: 2150-8097.

[3] L. Chang, W. Li, X. Lin, L. Qin, and W. Zhang, "pSCAN: Fast and Exact Structural Graph Clustering," in *Proceedings of the 32th International Conference on Data Engineering (ICDE) May 16–20, 2016, Helsinki, Finland*, pp. 387–401, ISBN: 978-1-5090-2020-1.

[4] N. Chiba and T. Nishizeki, "Arboricity and Subgraph Listing Algorithms," *Society for Industrial and Applied Mathematics*, vol. 14(1), pp. 210–223, 1994, ISSN: 0097-5397.

[5] S. Even, *Graph Algorithms (2nd ed.)*. Cambridge University Press, 2011, ISBN: 978-0-521-73653-4, pp. 46–48.

[6] T. H. Cormen, C. E. Leiserson, and R. Rivest, *Introduction to Algorithms (1st ed.)*. MIT Press and McGraw-Hill, 1990, ISBN: 0-262-03141-8, See in particular Section 26.2, "The FloydWarshall algorithm", pp. 558–565.

TOPSIS Assisted Selections of the Best Suited Universities for College Applications in Mainland China

Shan Lu and Jie Wang
Department of Computer Science
University of Massachusetts
Lowell, MA 01854, USA
Email: {slu, wang}@cs.uml.edu

***Abstract*—College admissions in mainland China depend mainly on the scores of the standardized annual examination called Gaokao. Students submit a common application to their provincial Gaokao office, on which they are allowed to list a fixed and small number of universities and majors they intend to study. The admission process in a province follows one of the following three admission models: parallel, gradient, and a combination of both. No matter what admission models are used, there is always a possibility that an applicant could end up being rejected by every university listed in the application, even though the applicant could have been accepted by a university not in the list. This process presents a challenge for students to figure out how to select universities to apply so that they can be admitted by a university and major that match their abilities and interests. To many students, and their parents, this is a difficult decision to make and their experience is unpleasant. To help reduce this agony, we present a new approach of applying Technique for Order Preference by Similarity to an Ideal Solution (TOPSIS) to generate a personalized selection of the best suited universities and majors that match a student's Gaokao score and meet a list of criteria. We then present case studies to demonstrate the effectiveness of this approach.**

Keywords–TOPSIS; weighted criteria; multi-attribute decision making; recommendation system

I. Introduction

Gaokao is the standardized annual examination for college entrance in mainland China, which takes place in early June every year. It is mandatory for admission into four-year colleges and universities. Each year during the last 10 years, there were over 9 (sometimes over 10) million high-school graduating students participating in Gaokao according to Chinese Education Online (http://gaokao.eol.cn/). Students must choose one of the two types of exams; namely the Li-Ke exam (meaning the science exam) and the Wen-Ke exam (meaning the liberal-arts exam). The Li-Ke exam must be taken by students for entering the disciplines of science, engineering, agriculture, and medicine; and the Wen-Ke exam must be taken by students for entering the disciplines of arts, humanity, education, and management. Students find out their Gaokao scores in late June, followed by the application and admission process that would last from one to two months.

Students in the same province must complete a common application form either prior to taking Gaokao or after, depending on the province or municipality in which they have official residency. A municipality is a very large city directly under the central government and so is treated as a province.

When the admission process starts, each application is released to a university selected from the universities listed in the application according to certain rules. That is, not all universities listed in an application can see the application simultaneously. If the university that receives the application rejects it, then the application is released to the next university in the list. However, this university may have already filled out its admission quota by then. Recall that students are only allowed to list a fixed and small number of universities and majors on their application forms. Thus, in addition to obtaining good Gaokao scores, students need to figure out which universities and majors they should apply to maximize their chances of acceptance while meeting their education goals. Note that each student can only be accepted by one university, or not accepted at all. This process is fundamentally different from the US where students may apply to universities directly as many as they would like and receive acceptance from multiple universities.

In mainland China, universities are officially categorized into three tiers based on the qualities and the number of programs they offer. National universities are the first tier, provincial universities are the second tier, and regional universities are the third tier. There are about 120 first-tier, 750 second-tier, and 1,550 third-tier universities. Applicants need to specify their preferences according to the official categorization.

Each university sets an admission quota for each province each year, which is broken down into majors. Each province sets its own rules on how universities access applications. These rules may be grouped into three admission models: parallel admission, gradient admission, and hybrid admission.

Mismatched admissions is a common problem. That is, if applicants apply to universities inappropriately, they may end up receiving no offer or an offer that is a poor match of their abilities or interests even though they could have been accepted by a university that presents a better match.

Both Gaokao and college admission are conducted only once a year. Once a student is admitted by a university to a particular major, it is almost impossible to change majors after admission. Thus, it is important to identify best-suited universities and majors to apply to, and students must complete their applications in a short period of time after Gaokao. To help reduce this agony, Lu, Zhang, and Wang [1] presented an automated system using General Morphological Analysis (GMA), based on a proprietary mathematical model for predicting admission scores for each major of each university in the current year, to analyze a large volume of data from previous years of Gaokao and help students make informed decisions based on their Gaokao scores and interests.

GMA is a method for identifying and investigating the total set of configurations contained in multi-dimensional, non-quantifiable problem complexes. It is "totality research" that attempts to derive all the solutions of any given problem in an unbiased manner. For a given admission model, we use GMA to identify suitable universities and majors for a student based on the student's Gaokao score and interests [1]. However, GMA does not allow students to specify weights over each interest they are interested to compute the best-suited university and major for the students. We present in this paper a method using Technique for Order Preference by Similarity to an Ideal Solution(TOPSIS) to fill this void. In particular, based on the universities and majors recommended by GMA for a student, we allow the student to specify the weight for each attribute and then use TOPSIS to compute the best-suited university and major. TOPSIS is a method for multi-criteria decision making, which was originally developed by Hwang and Yoon in 1981 [2] with further developments by Yoon in 1987 [3] and Hwang, Lai and Liu in 1993 [4]. TOPSIS is based on the concept that the chosen alternative should have the shortest geometric distance from the positive ideal solution [5] and the longest geometric distance from the negative ideal solution [5]. It compensates aggregation and compares a set of alternatives by identifying weights for each criterion, normalising scores for each criterion, and calculating the geometric distance between each alternative and the ideal alternative. To the best of our knowledge, our study is the first to use TOPSIS to produce Gaokao recommendations.

The remainder of this paper is organized as follows. In Section II, we describe how we identify all the suited universities and majors using GMA. In Section III, we describe TOPSIS and use it to generate the best-suited universities and majors among the suitable solutions found using GMA. In Section IV, we present two case studies and conclude the paper in Section V.

II. Identify All the Suited Universities and Majors using GMA

Lu, Zhang, and Wang [1] used computer assisted GMA to compute all possible combinations of majors and universities that are for students at various degrees according to their Gaokao scores and their interests under the admission model in their province. Let LU denote the set of labels for university slots in an application form, J the number of universities a student is allowed to specify for each tier, and K the number of majors a student is allowed to specify for a university. For example, in application forms for students living in the Fujian province, $J = 4$ and $K = 6$.

For convenience, in what follows we will use Alice to represent a student and XYU to represent a university. Alice enters her Gaokao score and other information to obtain recommendations for X-universities, where $X \in LU$, and we call them X-recommendations. For example, when $J = 4$, we have A-, B-, C-, and D-recommendations, respectively. Universities listed in A-recommendations are competitive for Alice, but Alice still has a chance to be accepted. Universities listed in B-recommendations would present a good match of Alice's ability and interests, which means that Alice would have a good chance to be accepted. Universities listed in C-recommendations are conservative choices for Alice, which means that Alice would have a very good chance to be accepted. Universities listed in D-recommendations are the safest choices for Alice, which means that Alice would have a near 100% chance to be accepted.

The baseline GMA setting consists of 14 parameters, divided evenly into two groups, one group for students and one group for universities. Parameters in the student group are (1) Alice's Gaokao score; (2) the type of the exam that Alice takes; (3) the tier of the universities that Alice wants to attend; (4) locations where Alice wants to go to for college; (5) locations Alice does not want to go to for college; (6) Majors that Alice wants to study; (7) majors that Alice does not want to study.

Parameters in the university group are (1) the lowest admission score of XYU in the past year; (2) the type of majors that XYU offers; (3) XYU's official tier; (4) XYU's location; (5) the majors that XYU offers, including (when possible) the lowest, medium, and highest admission scores for each major in the past year, and the total number of expected enrollment for a major for the current year; (6) the ranking of XYU (the first-tier universities are ranked from 1 to 5 with 1 being the highest one; the second-tier universities are ranked from 6 to 7; and the third-tier universities have one rank of 8); (7) the total enrollment of XYU for the current year (When this number is not known, it uses last year's enrollment number).

III. Identifying the Best-Suited Universities and Majors Using TOPSIS

TOPSIS is a multi-objective decision making method over a hierarchical structure of alternatives with multiple criteria. At the top level is the optimization goal. The next level consists of a list of criteria, which may be decomposed further into several levers of sub-criteria. The bottom level consists of a list of alternatives to be measured against each criterion. The criteria can relate to any aspect of the decision making, tangible or intangible, carefully measured or roughly estimated, well-defined or poorly understood.

Based on the concept that the chosen alternative should have the shortest geometric distance from the positive ideal solution and the longest geometric distance from the negative ideal solution, TOPSIS compensates aggregation through comparisons of alternatives by identifying weights for each criterion, normalizing the scores for each criterion and calculating the geometric distance between each alternative and the ideal alternative, which is the best score in each criterion. TOPSIS allows tradeoffs between criteria, where a poor result in one criterion can be negated by a good result in another criterion. This provides a more realistic form of modeling than non-compensatory methods, which include or exclude alternative solutions based on hard cutoffs [6].

To use TOPSIS, we need to ensure that the criteria of attributes are either monotonically increasing or monotonically decreasing and use normalisation to compensate incongruous dimensions in multi-criteria problems [7][8].

A. Criteria

After using GMA to obtain all suitable combinations of majors and universities for Alice, we create an evaluation matrix consisting of m alternatives and n criteria, where the alternatives are universities (XYU) and majors suitable for Alice, and the criteria are listed below:

1) Academic environment: This is the academic atmosphere of the city where XYU is located. In this paper we use the number of universities in the city where XYU is located to represent academic environment.

2) Economy: This is the economic growth level of the city where XYU is located. The China Business Network Weekly publishes a ranked list of economic growth for all the cities in China every year. Cities are ranked from the first tier to the eighth tier according to their economic development, with the first being the best (such as Beijing, Shanghai, and Guangzhou).

3) Enrollment: This is the summation of the enrollment figures of all suitable majors of XYU.

4) Interest matching: This is the matching of Alice's favored majors with suitable majors of XYU. In mainland China, areas of studies are officially classified into a hierarchy of three classes. The Class-1 category consists of 11 general areas of studies: (1) Philosophy, (2) Economics, (3) Law, (4) Education, (5) Literature, (6) History, (7) Science, (8) Engineering, (9) Agriculture, (10) Medicine, (11) Management.

Each area in Class 1 (referred to as Class-1 subject) often consists of a number of subjects referred to as Class-2 subjects. For example, Science is a Class-1 subject, which consists of 12 Class-2 subjects: (1) Math, (2) Physics, (3) Chemistry, (4) Astronomy, (5) Geographical Sciences, (6) Atmospheric Sciences, (7) Ocean Sciences, (8) Geophysics, (9) Geology, (10) Biological Sciences, (11) Psychology, (12) Statistics.

Each Class-2 subject further consists of a few subdisciplines referred to as Class-3 subjects. For example, Math is a Class-2 subject, which consists of two Class-3 subjects: (1) Mathematics and Applied Mathematics, (2) Information and Computing Science. Each subject in any class is uniquely identified by a subject code.

We allow students to specify majors at the Class-1 level, Class-2 level (after Class 1 is specified), or the Class-3 level (after Class 2 is specified) [1]. Let (a, b, c) denote a specification of major, where a is a subject in Class 1 (which could be empty), b a subject in Class 2 (which could be empty), and c a subject in Class 3 (which could be empty). Note that if a is empty, then b and c must be empty. Likewise, if b is empty then c must be empty. Given a major specification (a, b, c) entered by s, we define the following terms:

1) We say that a *match* occurs at level 3 for student s with university u if one of the following conditions are satisfied:
    a) The university u offers c.
    b) The university u offers b, and c is empty (in this case, any Class-3 subject offered by u under b is deemed specified by s).
    c) The university u offers a, and b is empty (in this case, any Class-3 subject offered by u under a is deemed specified by s).
    d) The specification (a, b, c) is empty (in this case, any Class-3 subject offered by u is deemed specified by s).
2) We say that a *match* occurs at level 2 for student s with university u, if b is offered by u, but c (not empty) is not offered by u.
3) We say that a *match* occurs at level 1 for student s with university u, if a is offered by u, but b (not empty) is not offered by u.

In addition to matching majors, we would also like to put more weight on university u if it offers more majors under a given Class-2 subject, for it provides more related disciplines of studies for student s. For a particular Class-2 subject b, let n_b denote the number of Class-3 majors u offers under b.

5) Ranking: This is the group ranking of XYU. The first-tier universities are characterized into five groups: Group G_1 consists of the two super universities: Peking University and Tsinghua University. They are the best funded and most reputable universities in China. Both universities are designated by the Chinese government as project-985 universities. There are 39 universities in mainland China with this designation, which are the national key universities; Group G_2 consists of the top ten universities after Peking and Tsinghua. They are also project-985 universities. Group G_3 consists of all the remaining 27 project-985 universities; Group G_4 consists of all the officially designated project-211 universities, excluding project-985 universities. These are universities having top programs in certain areas; Group G_5 consists of the remaining first-tier universities. The second-tier universities can also be further characterized into two groups: Group G_6 consists of provincial key universities; Group G_7 consists of the remaining universities in this tier. Group G_8 consists of all the universities in the third tier.

B. Weights

Alice enters a weight value w_j for each criterion C_j, where $w_j \in \{0, 1, \ldots, 10\}$ with the following meanings: 0 is to ignore this criterion; 2 is to consider this criterion with no importance, 4 is moderately important; 6 is strongly important, 8 is very strongly important, 10 is extremely important, and 1, 3, 5, 7, 9 are between the above scales.

C. TOPSIS Steps

Step 1. Create an evaluation matrix U with universities as alternatives and the criteria set up above.

$$U = \begin{matrix} & C_1 & C_2 & \cdots & C_n \\ A_1 & u_{1,1} & u_{1,2} & \cdots & u_{1,n} \\ A_2 & u_{2,1} & u_{2,2} & \cdots & u_{2,n} \\ \vdots & \vdots & \vdots & \ddots & \vdots \\ A_m & u_{m,1} & u_{m,2} & \cdots & u_{m,n} \end{matrix}$$

Step 2. Normalize matrix U to form the matrix $R = (r_{ij})_{m \times n}$, where for $i = 1, 2, \ldots, m$ and $j = 1, 2, \ldots, n$,

$$r_{ij} = u_{ij} \left(\sum_{i=1}^{m} \sum_{j=1}^{n} u_{ij}^2 \right)^{-1/2}. \quad (1)$$

Step 3. Normalize weights entered by Alice such that the new weights, still denoted by w_j for criterion C_j with $j = 1, \ldots, n$, satisfies $\sum_{j=1}^{n} w_j = 1$. This is often referred to as linear normalization.

Step 4. Multiply the weights to each of the column entries in the matrix R to obtain a new matrix $T = (t_{ij})$, where $t_{ij} = w_i r_{ij}$, for $i = 1, 2, \ldots, m$ and $j = 1, 2, \ldots, n$. That is,

$$T = \begin{pmatrix} w_1 r_{1,1} & w_2 r_{1,2} & \cdots & w_n r_{1,n} \\ w_1 r_{2,1} & w_2 r_{2,2} & \cdots & w_n r_{2,n} \\ \vdots & \vdots & \ddots & \vdots \\ w_1 r_{m,1} & w_2 r_{m,2} & \cdots & w_n r_{m,n} \end{pmatrix}$$

Step 5. Determine the best alternative vector, denoted by $\boldsymbol{A}_b$; and the worst alternative vector, denoted by $\boldsymbol{A}_w$. Write

$$\boldsymbol{A}_b = (t_{b1}, t_{b2}, \ldots, t_{bn})^T, \tag{2}$$

$$\boldsymbol{A}_w = (t_{w1}, t_{w2}, \ldots, t_{wn})^T. \tag{3}$$

Let $J_- = \{j \mid C_j \text{ is the smaller the better}, j = 1, \ldots, n\}$ and $J_+ = \{j \mid C_j \text{ is the larger the better}, j = 1, \ldots, n\}$. Then for $j = 1, 2, \ldots, n$,

$$t_{bj} = \begin{cases} \max\{t_{ij} \mid i = 1, 2, \ldots, m\}, & \text{if } C_j \in J_+, \\ \min\{t_{ij} \mid i = 1, 2, \ldots, m\}, & \text{if } C_j \in J_-; \end{cases} \tag{4}$$

$$t_{wj} = \begin{cases} \min\{t_{ij} \mid i = 1, 2, \ldots, m\}, & \text{if } C_j \in J_+, \\ \max\{t_{ij} \mid i = 1, 2, \ldots, m\}, & \text{if } C_j \in J_-. \end{cases} \tag{5}$$

Step 6. For each alternative A_i with $1 \le i \le m$, calculate the Euclidean distance between $(t_{i,1}, t_{i,2}, \cdots, t_{i,n})^T$ and $\boldsymbol{A}_b$, denoted by d_{ib}, and between $(t_{i,1}, t_{i,2}, \cdots, t_{i,n})^T$ and $\boldsymbol{A}_w$, denoted by d_{iw}, as follows: $d_{ib} = \sqrt{\sum_{j=1}^{n} (t_{ij} - t_{bj})^2}$, and $d_{iw} = \sqrt{\sum_{j=1}^{n} (t_{ij} - t_{wj})^2}$, where $i = 1, 2, \cdots, m$.

Step 7. For each alternative A_i, calculate the similarity to A_w as follows:

$$s_{iw} = d_{iw} / (d_{ib} + d_{iw}), \tag{6}$$

where $0 \le s_{iw} \le 1$, $i = 1, 2, \cdots, m$. The alternative A_i with the largest value s_{iw} is the best alternative. In other words, that university is the optimal one for Alice.

IV. Case Studies

We present two case studies, where Tom and Bob are high school seniors in the JiangSu Province. In JiangSu, each student must select two subjects from Politics, History, Physics, Chemistry, Geology, Biology, and Technology; and take them in addition to the must-take Gaokao subjects of Chinese, Mathematics, and English. The two selected subjects will be graded with a letter grade for A+, A, B+, B, C, or D. The three Gaokao subjects are graded numerically. Students who take the Li-Ke exam must choose Physics and students who take the Wen-Ke exam must choose History in their two selected subjects, respectively. Note that the selected subjects are criteria for GMA, not for TOPSIS. For a student to be admitted to a university, a good Gaokao score and good grades of selected subjects are a must. We will analyze the first-tier optimal recommendation for Tom and the second-tier optimal recommendation for Bob using TOPSIS, and justify that they make sense. We use data in the year of 2015 for demonstration.

A. Case A

Tom obtains a Gaokao score of 407 in the Li-Ke exam and A+ for both of his selected subjects. He is not interested in Literature, Economics, Law, Medicine, Management or Engineering, and he likes to study in Beijing or the Hubei province. The weights he gives to academic environment, economy, enrollment, interest matching, and ranking are 5, 4, 1, 1, and 7.

For the 2015 Gaokao in the Jiangsu province, the highest mark in the Li-Ke exam was 425 out of 480 (the student with this mark went to Tsinghua University) and the highest mark in the Wen-Ke exam was 418 out of 480 (the student with this mark went to Peking University). The mark of 407 in the Li-Ke exam was ranked from the 80th to the 94th among about 180,000 students who took the Li-Ke exams. Students in this range were admitted to top universities including University of Chinese Academy of Sciences and Renmin University of China in Beijing; and Wuhan University and Huazhong University of Science and Technology in Hubei. Table I shows the values for TOPSIS on the following universities recommended by GMA based on Tom's Gaokao score and interests, where AE stands for Academic Environment, IM for Interest Matching:

- China Agricultural University (CAU),
- Huazhong University of Science and Technology (HUST),
- University of Chinese Academy of Sciences (UCAS),
- Beijing Institute of Technology (BIT),
- Beijing University of Posts and Telecommunications (BUPT),
- Beihang University (BHU),
- North China Electric Power University (NCEPU),
- Wuhan University (WU),
- Central University of Finance and Economics (CUFE),
- Beijing Normal University (BNU),
- Renmin University of China (RUC),
- Zhongnan University of Economics and Law (ZUEL).

TABLE I. UNIVERSITY VALUES FOR TOPSIS

University	AE	Economy	Enrollment	IM	Ranking
CAU	10.0	10.0	1.0	10.0	7.50
HUST	10.0	7.50	2.0	10.0	7.50
UCAS	10.0	10.0	1.0	10.0	5.00
BIT	10.0	10.0	2.0	10.0	7.50
BUPT	10.0	10.0	1.0	10.0	6.25
BHU	10.0	10.0	2.0	10.0	7.50
NCEPU	10.0	10.0	1.0	10.0	6.25
WU	10.0	7.50	4.0	10.0	8.75
CUFE	10.0	10.0	1.0	10.0	6.25
BNU	10.0	10.0	2.0	10.0	7.50
RUC	10.0	10.0	1.0	10.0	8.75
ZUEL	10.0	7.50	1.0	10.0	6.25

Tables II and III represent, respectively, the linear normalization and criterion weight normalization. Table IV represents the process of multiplying the weights to each of the column entries in the normalized matrix of university values for TOPSIS. Tables V and VI show the best alternative vector and the worst alternative vector, respectively. Table VII displays the Euclidean distance between alternatives and the best alternative vector, and the worst alternative vector, respectively. Table VIII shows the similarities to the worst possible alternatives.

From Table VIII, we can see that RUC (Renmin University of China) in Beijing has the largest value. From Table II, we can see that RUC has the top score for each criterion except Enrollment, and from Table III, we can see that Tom cares more about Ranking, Academic Environment, and Economy, and he does not care much about Enrollment or Interest Matching. Thus, all things considered, we conclude that RUC is the best-suited university for Tom to apply. Based on the admission data in 2015, we confirm that RUC did admit students with Gaokao scores similar to Tom's.

TABLE II. NORMALIZED MATRIX OF UNIVERSITY VALUES FOR TOPSIS

University	AE	Economy	Enrollment	IM	Ranking
CAU	0.0389	0.0311	8.0E-4	0.0078	0.0409
HUST	0.0389	0.0234	0.0016	0.0078	0.0409
UCAS	0.0389	0.0311	8.0E-4	0.0078	0.0273
BIT	0.0389	0.0311	0.0016	0.0078	0.0409
BUPT	0.0389	0.0311	8.0E-4	0.0078	0.0341
BHU	0.0389	0.0311	0.0016	0.0078	0.0409
NCEPU	0.0389	0.0311	8.0E-4	0.0078	0.0341
WU	0.0389	0.0234	0.0031	0.0078	0.0477
CUFE	0.0389	0.0311	8.0E-4	0.0078	0.0341
BNU	0.0389	0.0311	0.0016	0.0078	0.0409
RUC	0.0389	0.0311	8.0E-4	0.0078	0.0477
ZUEL	0.0389	0.0234	8.0E-4	0.0078	0.0341

TABLE III. NORMALIZED CRITERION WEIGHTS

Criterion number	Criterion name	Normalized criterion weight
1	Academic Environment	0.25
2	Economy	0.20
3	Enrollment	0.05
4	Interest Matching	0.05
5	Ranking	0.35

TABLE IV. NORMALIZED WEIGHTED DATA

University	AE	Economy	Enrollment	IM	Ranking
CAU	0.0389	0.0311	8.0E-4	0.0078	0.0409
HUST	0.0389	0.0234	0.0016	0.0078	0.0409
UCAS	0.0389	0.0311	8.0E-4	0.0078	0.0273
BIT	0.0389	0.0311	0.0016	0.0078	0.0409
BUPT	0.0389	0.0311	8.0E-4	0.0078	0.0341
BHU	0.0389	0.0311	0.0016	0.0078	0.0409
NCEPU	0.0389	0.0311	8.0E-4	0.0078	0.0341
WU	0.0389	0.0234	0.0031	0.0078	0.0477
CUFE	0.0389	0.0311	8.0E-4	0.0078	0.0341
BNU	0.0389	0.0311	0.0016	0.0078	0.0409
RUC	0.0389	0.0311	8.0E-4	0.0078	0.0477
ZUEL	0.0389	0.0234	8.0E-4	0.0078	0.0341

TABLE V. THE BEST POSSIBLE

AE	Economy	Enrollment	IM	Ranking
0.0389	0.0311	0.0031	0.0078	0.0477

TABLE VI. THE WORST POSSIBLE

AE	Economy	Enrollment	IM	Ranking
0.0389	0.0234	8.0E-4	0.0078	0.0273

TABLE VII. DISTANCE TO THE BEST POSSIBLE (DTBP) AND THE DISTANCE TO THE WORST POSSIBLE (DTWP)

University	DTBP	DTWP
CAU	0.0072	0.0157
HUST	0.0105	0.0136
UCAS	0.0206	0.0078
BIT	0.0070	0.0157
BUPT	0.0138	0.0103
BHU	0.0070	0.0157
NCEPU	0.0138	0.0103
WU	0.0078	0.0206
CUFE	0.0138	0.0103
BNU	0.0070	0.0157
RUC	0.0023	0.0219
ZUEL	0.0159	0.0068

B. Case B

Bob's Gaokao score is 375 in the Wen-Ke exam and his two selected subjects are both B. Recall that the full mark

TABLE VIII. SIMILARITY TO THE WORST POSSIBLE (STWP)

University	STWP
CAU	0.6854
HUST	0.5661
UCAS	0.2746
BIT	0.6922
BUPT	0.4280
BHU	0.6922
NCEPU	0.4280
WU	0.7254
CUFE	0.4280
BNU	0.6922
RUC	0.9035
ZUEL	0.3004

of the Wen-Ke exam in 2015 was 480 and the highest mark was 418. He is interested in Literature but not in Agronomy, Medicine, Management, Law, or Economics. He likes to study in the Jiangsu province, Liaoning province, or Shanghai. He enters the following weights of 4, 2, 4, 5, 3 on Academic Environment, Economy, Enrollment, Interest Matching, and Ranking.

Bob's Gaokao score in the Wen-Ke exam in 2015 was ranked from the 754th to the 834th. Students with Gaokao scores in this range were admitted by Shanghai Normal University, Nanjing University of Posts and Telecommunications in Jiangsu, and Dalian University of Foreign Languages in Liaoning. Table IX shows the university values for TOPSIS on the following universities recommended by GMA:

- Shanghai Second Polytechnic University (SSPU),
- Nanjing Technical University (NTU),
- Shanghai Customs College (SCC),
- Nanjing University of Posts and Telecommunications (NUPT),
- Shanghai University of Political Science and Law (SUPSL),
- Shanghai Normal University (SNU),
- Yangzhou University (YU),
- Shanghai Finance University (SFU),
- Nantong University (NU),
- Dalian University of Foreign Languages (DUFL),
- Shanghai Lixin University of Accounting and Finance (SLUAF),
- Shanghai Ocean University (SOU).

TABLE IX. UNIVERSITY VALUES FOR TOPSIS

University	AE	Economic level	Enrollment	IM	Ranking
SSPU	10.0	10.0	1.00	9.79	3.75
NTU	10.0	8.75	1.00	9.79	5.00
SCC	10.0	10.0	1.00	9.79	3.75
NUPT	10.0	8.75	6.00	10.0	5.00
SUPSL	10.0	10.0	2.00	10.0	2.50
SNU	10.0	10.0	1.00	9.79	3.75
YU	1.04	5.00	10.0	10.0	5.00
SFU	10.0	10.0	1.00	9.79	3.75
NU	1.11	5.00	2.00	9.79	3.75
DUFL	5.85	8.75	2.00	10.0	3.75
SLUAF	10.0	10.0	1.00	9.79	2.50
SOU	10.0	10.0	1.00	9.79	2.50

Table X shows linear normalization. Table XI displays criterion weight normalization. Table XII represents the process of multiplying the weights to each of the column entries in the normalized matrix of university values for TOPSIS. Tables XIII and XIV show the best alternative vector and the worst alternative vector, respectively. Table XV shows, respectively, the Euclidean distance between alternatives and the best alternative vector, and the worst alternative vector. Table XVI shows the similarity to the worst possible alternatives.

TABLE X. NORMALIZED MATRIX

University	AE	Economy	Enrollment	IM	Ranking
SSPU	0.1711	0.1711	0.0171	0.1675	0.0642
NTU	0.1711	0.1497	0.0171	0.1675	0.0855
SCC	0.1711	0.1711	0.0171	0.1675	0.0642
NUPT	0.1711	0.1497	0.1027	0.1711	0.0855
SUPSL	0.1711	0.1711	0.0342	0.1711	0.0428
SNU	0.1711	0.1711	0.0171	0.1675	0.0642
YU	0.0177	0.0855	0.1711	0.1711	0.0855
SFU	0.1711	0.1711	0.0171	0.1675	0.0642
NU	0.0190	0.0855	0.0342	0.1675	0.0642
DUFL	0.1001	0.1497	0.0342	0.1711	0.0642
SLUAF	0.1711	0.1711	0.0171	0.1675	0.0428
SOU	0.1711	0.1711	0.0171	0.1675	0.0428

TABLE XI. NORMALIZED CRITERION WEIGHTS

Criterion number	Criterion name	Normalized criterion weight
1	Academic Atmosphere	0.20
2	Economic Level	0.10
3	Enrollment	0.20
4	Interest Matching	0.25
5	Ranking	0.15

TABLE XII. NORMALIZED WEIGHTED DATA

University	AE	Economy	Enrollment	IM	Ranking
SSPU	0.0342	0.0171	0.0034	0.0419	0.0128
NTU	0.0342	0.0150	0.0034	0.0419	0.0128
SCC	0.0342	0.0171	0.0034	0.0419	0.0096
NUPT	0.0342	0.0150	0.0205	0.0428	0.0128
SUPSL	0.0342	0.0171	0.0068	0.0428	0.0064
SNU	0.0342	0.0171	0.0034	0.0419	0.0096
YU	0.0035	0.0086	0.0342	0.0428	0.0128
SFU	0.0342	0.0171	0.0034	0.0419	0.0096
NU	0.0038	0.0086	0.0068	0.0419	0.0096
DUFL	0.0200	0.0150	0.0068	0.0428	0.0096
SLUAF	0.0342	0.0171	0.0034	0.0419	0.0064
SOU	0.0342	0.0171	0.0034	0.0419	0.0064

TABLE XIII. THE BEST POSSIBLE

AE	Economy	Enrollment	IM	Ranking
0.0342	0.0171	0.0342	0.0428	0.0128

TABLE XIV. THE WORST POSSIBLE

AE	Economy	Enrollment	IN	Ranking
0.0035	0.0086	0.0034	0.0419	0.0064

From Table XVIII, we can see that NUPT (Nanjing University of Posts and Telecommunications) has the largest value. From Table XI, we can see that NUPT has the top score for all the criteria except Economy. From Table XII, we can see that Bob cares more about other criteria than Economy. Thus, we can conclude that NUPT is the best-suited university for Bob to apply. Based on the admission data in 2015, we confirm that NUPT did admit students with Gaokao scores similar to Bob's.

TABLE XV. DISTANCE TO THE BEST POSSIBLE (DTBP) AND DISTANCE TO THE WORST POSSIBLE (DTWP)

University	DTBP	DTWP
SSPU	0.0310	0.0320
NTU	0.0309	0.0320
SCC	0.0310	0.0320
NUPT	0.0139	0.0363
SUPSL	0.0281	0.0320
SNU	0.0310	0.0320
YU	0.0318	0.0315
SFU	0.0310	0.0320
NU	0.0419	0.0047
DUFL	0.0311	0.0183
SLUAF	0.0315	0.0318
SOU	0.0315	0.0318

TABLE XVI. SIMILARITY TO THE WORST POSSIBLE (STWP)

University	STWP
SSPU	0.5081
NTU	0.5088
SCC	0.5081
NUPT	0.7237
SUPSL	0.5326
SNU	0.5081
YU	0.4971
SFU	0.5081
NU	0.1007
DUFL	0.3708
SLUAF	0.5029
SOU	0.5029

V. Conclusion and Future Work

Gaokao is a unique and major annual event in mainland China, which affects the lives of about 10 million graduating high-school students each year, and attracts tremendous attentions by their parents, relatives, and teachers. We presented an automated tool using computer assisted TOPSIS over big data to identify the best-suited university that matches the student's Gaokao score and interests. Our case studies showed that the recommendation provided by TOPSIS makes sense. Using computer assisted TOPSIS, students can easily figure out the best universities to apply under different sets of weights for the criteria. In a future project, we plan to fully develop this tool by allowing students to specify their own criteria.

References

[1] S. Lu, H. Zhang, and J. Wang, "EEZY: A Gaokao Recommendation System Using General Morphological Analysis over Big Data." Journal of Acta Morphologica Generalis, vol. 12, 2016, pp. 5(1): 1–12, ISSN: 2001-2241.

[2] C. L. Hwang and K. Yoon, Multiple Attribute Decision Making: Methods and Applications. New York: Springer-Verlag, 1981.

[3] K. Yoon, "A reconciliation among discrete compromise situations." Journal of Operational Research Society, vol. 10, 1987, pp. 277–286.

[4] C. L. Hwang, Y. Lai, and T. Liu, "A new approach for multiple objective decision making." Computers and Operational Research, vol. 11, 1993, pp. 20:889–899.

[5] A. Assari, T. Mahesh, and E. Assari, " Role of public participation in sustainability of historical city: usage of TOPSIS method." Indian Journal of Science and Technology, vol. 6, 2012, pp. 5(3), 2289–2294.

[6] R. Greene, R. Devillers, J. Luther, and B. Eddy, "GIS-based multi-criteria analysis." Geography Compass, vol. 21, 2006, p. 5/6: 412432.

[7] E. Zavadskas, A. Zakarevicius, and J. Antucheviciene, " Evaluation of Ranking Accuracy in Multi-Criteria Decisions." Journal of Informatica, vol. 18, 2006, p. 17 (4): 601618.

[8] K. Yoon and C. Hwang, Multiple Attribute Decision Making: An Introduction. California: SAGE publications., 1995.

AUTHOR INDEX